REBUILD THE WALLS

Lessons in Leadership from Nehemiah

Loren VanGalder

Spiritual Father Publications

Contents

Introduction

What can one man do? You may be alarmed at things you see happening in your family. You may feel helpless as you hear of tragedies around the world. But you have the potential to be a world changer. Look at eighty-year-old Moses. Who would have thought someone exiled to the backside of the desert for forty years would deliver his entire nation from slavery? History is full of men and women who have made a difference.

Nehemiah shows what one man can do in the face of calamity. Even though he held an important position, Nehemiah was still a captive - a prisoner - in Babylon. He faced huge obstacles, but through his faith in God he overcame them. We need men like Nehemiah today. Of course we all have different gifts and callings, but God can do amazing things through you. *With his help you can rebuild walls and change the world.*

Chapter 1

Responding to Devastation
Nehemiah 1

¹The words of Nehemiah son of Hakaliah:

In the month of Kislev in the twentieth year, while I was in the citadel of Susa, ² Hanani, one of my brothers, came from Judah with some other men, and I questioned them about the Jewish remnant that had survived the exile, and also about Jerusalem.

It's important to know what's going on in your family, the Body of Christ, and the world. In Nehemiah's day it could take months to get news from back home. Today it's immediate. TMI has become a common expression. Too much information. We can get overloaded to the point that we tune it out. It's easy to get caught up in daily life and not want to be bothered with somebody else's suffering. Nehemiah had no need to worry about what was happening in Jerusalem. He was enjoying a good life in the king's palace, yet he refused to fall into complacency.

³ They said to me, "Those who survived the exile and are back in the province are in great trouble and disgrace. The wall of Jerusalem is broken down, and its gates have been burned with fire. "

How do you respond to bad news from your family, or news of yet another disaster? Does it touch your heart? Or do you try to stay emotionally detached? How does your response compare with Nehemiah's?

Responding to bad news

⁴ When I heard these things, I sat down and wept. For some days I mourned and fasted and prayed before the God of heaven.

God calls us to take the news seriously – and do something. What did Nehemiah do?

1. He sat down and wept. When was the last time you actually wept when you heard bad news?

2. He mourned. Way beyond just feeling bad, he was seriously impacted. It's good to feel others' pain. God does. Resist the temptation to dismiss it with trite sayings like "It's God's will," or "God is judging their sin," or "Thank you, Lord, that I don't live there."

3. He didn't rush it. This went on for "some days." It's easy to see something, feel bad for a while,

and then get busy with other things. Nehemiah wanted the situation to touch him deeply.

4. He fasted. How's your fasting going? When was the last time you fasted after hearing about problems Christians are facing in other countries? A fast declares: "I'm taking this seriously, and I know Jesus is the answer."

5. He prayed. It's dangerous to respond impulsively. Whatever we do must be directed by the Lord. We have to be spiritually prepared or we won't be able to help anyone. We have to work with God.

5 Then I said: "Lord, the God of heaven, the great and awesome God, who keeps his covenant of love with those who love him and keep his commandments, 6 let your ear be attentive and your eyes open to hear the prayer your servant is praying before you day and night for your servants, the people of Israel.

A man God uses

Nehemiah knows his God, loves him, and obeys him. He confidently comes before him in bold prayer. Whether it's in your family or across the globe, a calamity demands more than a few minutes of prayer. Like Paul praying without ceasing, it calls for day and night intercession.

⁶ I confess the sins we Israelites, including myself and my father's family, have committed against you. ⁷ We have acted very wickedly toward you. We have not obeyed the commands, decrees and laws you gave your servant Moses.

At the same time he's humble. He knows he's a sinner who has failed God and deserves his judgment, the same judgment Nehemiah's people are now experiencing. He knows rebellion and sin have caused the problems. He confesses his sin and the sin of the nation. When you see sin in the church, do you judge the offender in your heart? Or do you identify as part of the church, and confess the sin to God?

God's promise to the repentant

⁸ "Remember the instruction you gave your servant Moses, saying, 'If you are unfaithful, I will scatter you among the nations, ⁹ but if you return to me and obey my commands, then even if your exiled people are at the farthest horizon, I will gather them from there and bring them to the place I have chosen as a dwelling for my Name.'

Nehemiah knows the Word of God and bases his request on it. The promise made to Moses still applies today. If you are unfaithful, there will be grave consequences. You will lose your home and all that matters to you. In that place of judgment God calls you to do two things:

1. Return to him with all your heart. Seek him once
    again.

2. Obey his commands. Genuine repentance is
    evidenced by obedience and living out the Word.
    Biblical knowledge abounds, even outside the
    church, but few put it into practice.

If you do that, God promises to restore you and take you
back to his dwelling place.

Are you still suffering the consequences of your sin? Has
God gathered you back to a place of rest and blessing?
Are you dwelling in his presence? Israel's restoration
wasn't immediate. They had to wait and work for it, but
God is faithful to his promise.

It's all about God's grace

[10] *"They are your servants and your people, whom you
redeemed by your great strength and your mighty hand.*
[11] *Lord, let your ear be attentive to the prayer of this your
servant and to the prayer of your servants who delight in
revering your name. Give your servant success today by
granting him favor in the presence of this man."*

When you intercede for the church, remember they're
God's people and *his* servants. God is obligated to act on
their behalf. He's already bought them with his Son's
blood. Nehemiah has nothing to gain here, but he's
God's servant and wants to honor him. He may have

been the only one in Israel interceding, and the only one in a position to do something. It appears the Lord already put in his heart what to do.

11 I was cupbearer to the king.

The cupbearer tasted drinks to see if they might be poisoned. It was a position of great trust. Nehemiah may have spent years thinking "What am I doing here? I'm not doing anything to help my people. I'm wasting my life tasting wine for this oppressive king!" But God had put him there for a time like this.

Where has God placed you? Are you in a position of influence? Are you praying about how the Lord wants to use you in that position?

Today we're accosted on TV and the internet by news of tragedies all over the world. It's easy to be overwhelmed and fall into despair. We must keep our eyes on Jesus and resist a hardened heart. If every Christian had Nehemiah's attitude and did something to change the situation, our world would be transformed.

Chapter 2

A Twelve Step Program for World Changers
Nehemiah 2:1-10

God takes a prisoner, puts him in a key position in his oppressor's palace, and sends him to rebuild the walls of Jerusalem, and, more importantly, its people.

Like Joseph. In the morning he was a prisoner and by evening the second most powerful man in Egypt.

Like you.

Why not? If you serve the same God, why can't he do the same with you?

How did Nehemiah do it? Here are twelve simple, biblical, steps to get you ready to change your world:

1. **Prepare yourself spiritually.** The prayer and fasting in chapter one laid the foundation. Nehemiah got in line with God's plan. When you're in sync with the Lord of the universe, his power and favor start to flow. That was

a key premise of the *Experiencing God* study that was so popular several years ago.

¹In the month of Nisan in the twentieth year of King Artaxerxes, when wine was brought for him, I took the wine and gave it to the king. I had not been sad in his presence before.

2. **Continue your daily life as usual.** Work, and fulfill your other obligations. Do everything with excellence. It helps when your job brings you in daily contact with the king. God has a way of moving his people into positions of influence. Consider that as you think about options for your future, although God can use you anywhere.

3. **Maintain an outstanding testimony.** Could your boss say he's never seen you sad? How about your family? There are lots of sad believers out there, and everyone sees it. Not that a Christian can never be sad, but it's a great testimony when we can maintain the joy of the Lord in hard times. Nehemiah had always been upbeat in the king's presence, and he noticed it. Nehemiah could say "the joy of the Lord is your strength" from personal experience.

² So the king asked me, "Why does your face look so sad when you are not ill? This can be nothing but sadness of heart."

4. **Develop good relationships - with everyone** (See Romans 12:18, I Timothy 3:7). The king's concern shows

that Nehemiah was close to him, even though he was a slave. Demonstrate Christ's love in your compassion and interest in your superiors and co-workers. Does it matter to you if they're sad, or sick?

5. **Wait for God's timing.** Some four months had passed since his fast. Don't get impatient and try to make something happen in your own strength. Trust in the Lord to provide the opportunity.

²I was very much afraid, ³ but I said to the king, "May the king live forever! Why should my face not look sad when the city where my ancestors are buried lies in ruins, and its gates have been destroyed by fire?"

6. **When the Lord opens the door, go through it.** Honestly share what's on your heart. Nehemiah knows he's a slave, and has struggled to maintain a healthy self-image. You may wait months for the door to open – and then be afraid when it does. That's okay, but step out in faith anyway. When someone asks why you're always happy, tell them the truth: it's Jesus who makes the difference in your life.

⁴ The king said to me, "What is it you want?"

7. **When you do your part, trusting in God, the Lord will touch others.** Even the king. Proverbs 21:1 says *In the Lord's hand the king's heart is a stream of water that he channels toward all who please him.*

⁴Then I prayed to the God of heaven, ⁵ and I answered the king, "If it pleases the king and if your servant has found favor in his sight, let him send me to the city in Judah where my ancestors are buried so that I can rebuild it."

⁶ Then the king, with the queen sitting beside him, asked me, "How long will your journey take, and when will you get back?"

8. **Keep your eyes on the Lord, and keep praying.** It has nothing to do with your persuasive words or convincing presentation. Nehemiah bathed everything he did in prayer. He knows he needs favor with God - and the king - to complete this task.

9. **When God opens the door, be ready.** Know exactly what you want to do and what you need to do it. Speak confidently and clearly. Nehemiah had prayed, and has a very ambitious plan: He wants to rebuild the city of his ancestors. What can you do to rebuild what the enemy has destroyed in your family and church?

⁶It pleased the king to send me; so I set a time. ⁷ I also said to him, "If it pleases the king, may I have letters to the governors of Trans-Euphrates, so that they will provide me safe-conduct until I arrive in Judah? ⁸ And may I have a letter to Asaph, keeper of the royal park, so he will give me timber to make beams for the gates of the citadel by the temple and for the city wall and for the residence I will occupy?"

10. **This is not the time to be shy.** God is with you! Ask for everything God has put in your heart – but no more. Don't get in the flesh and decide to throw in things for yourself which God never mentioned. Nehemiah tested the waters, and when he saw God moving, and the king's positive response, he gets bolder and asks for more. When God leads you to do something and his favor is with you, ask big, whether it's from the government or wealthy individuals.

[8] And because the gracious hand of my God was on me, the king granted my requests. [9] So I went to the governors of Trans-Euphrates and gave them the king's letters. The king had also sent army officers and cavalry with me.

11. **Don't be surprised if God gives you more than you expected.** When he's moving in your favor, miracles happen. He will provide beyond what you can imagine, like the cavalry and army officers here.

[10]When Sanballat the Horonite and Tobiah the Ammonite official heard about this, they were very much disturbed that someone had come to promote the welfare of the Israelites.

12. **Be prepared for battle.** The enemy is furious when he sees God's hand on your life. Don't let it bother

you. There will always be opposition. If you've been given great resources and rise up in great faith to restore the church, the devil will do everything in his power to stop you. People will be jealous of you.

Who is your Sanballat and Tobiah right now? How are they affecting you? We'll see later how to deal with them. Fight fear and discouragement! Many fall apart here and lose the opportunity to do great things for the Lord. Take a serious look at these twelve steps. With God's help, couldn't they get you on the path to being a world changer?

Chapter 3

Ten Steps Further: Getting the People to Work
Nehemiah 2:11-20

God did a miracle. He took a prisoner from Babylon and brought him to Jerusalem with letters of safe conduct from the king, along with army officers and cavalry! He's given wood from the king's forests. He has his task, and the provisions for it, but he still hasn't done anything. He's just arrived. Unfortunately, there are countless people with dreams, a vision, and a call from God to do great things. But for some reason they never do anything.

So Nehemiah needs another miracle – and he gets it. People who've lived in ruins and disgrace for years get busy restoring their city. Nehemiah laid the foundation with the twelve steps in the last chapter. Now we'll see how God gets the people to work. Is your church or city in need of motivated people to work for the Lord? Could God use you to get them moving? Let's look at the next ten steps, to turn the dream into reality.

11 I went to Jerusalem, and after staying there three days
*12 I set out during the night with a few others. I had not
told anyone what my God had put in my heart to do for
Jerusalem. There were no mounts with me except the
one I was riding on.*

1. **There's no need to tell the whole world what God
has put in your heart, and no need to rush it.** Nehemiah
waited three days to settle in and observe what was
happening in the city. Many who receive a prophetic
word immediately announce it to everyone. It's like they
want to say: "I've arrived. God sent me here to help
you. I'm coming from the King of Assyria." It draws more
attention to the man than to God or the task.

Take good care of the treasures God has given you. Be
wise in how you share them. Not all are meant to be
shared. Remember Jesus' words in Matthew 7:6: *"Do not
give dogs what is sacred; do not throw your pearls to
pigs. If you do, they may trample them under their feet,
and turn and tear you to pieces."*

*13 By night I went out through the Valley Gate toward the
Jackal Well and the Dung Gate, examining the walls of
Jerusalem, which had been broken down, and its gates,
which had been destroyed by fire. 14 Then I moved on
toward the Fountain Gate and the King's Pool, but there
was not enough room for my mount to get through; 15 so
I went up the valley by night, examining the wall. Finally,
I turned back and reentered through the Valley Gate.*

2. **Study and evaluate the situation.** Inspect the church, the city, or the country to see what's happening in the spirit realm and how to approach the work. It's good to walk through a neighborhood, listening to discern God's heart. As Nehemiah walked the walls God may have been showing him what to do.

16 The officials did not know where I had gone or what I was doing, because as yet I had said nothing to the Jews or the priests or nobles or officials or any others who would be doing the work.

3. **Be careful sharing your vision with leaders.** A young man may tell a pastor his vision of something he wants to do in the church, but if he's not wise in how he does it, the pastor may feel threatened or respond negatively. Instead, the Lord might guide you to an elder who is more open, who could then speak with the pastor. And just like Nehemiah did before speaking to the king, make sure you're prepared. Pray over it. Be sure it's really from the Lord.

17 Then I said to them, "You see the trouble we are in: Jerusalem lies in ruins, and its gates have been burned with fire. Come, let us rebuild the wall of Jerusalem, and we will no longer be in disgrace. "

4. **When the time comes to speak to the leaders, follow Nehemiah's example:**

- Don't attempt to bypass them. Make them part of it, or you may run into serious resistance.

- Speak about what's obvious, a problem they've already recognized, before presenting a plan to deal with it.

- He includes himself in the problem: "We're in this together. I may have come from the king, but I'm one of you."

- Tell it like it is, so they see the need to do something. Often when you've lived in ruins for years, with your gates burned, you don't realize how bad it is anymore, like people who've been in a bad marriage for years. It's time for them to wake up and see things as they are.

- He doesn't blame them or question why they haven't done more. He comes with a positive message of hope and action. The truth is, all they needed was a leader, and Nehemiah's the man. It reminds me of Moses and the slaves in Egypt.

5. **This is not about Nehemiah making a name for himself.** He doesn't try to sell his plan by saying how good the leaders will look. This is about glorifying God. They're in disgrace! They're a laughing stock! Somebody has to do something for God and his people! Like David said in 1 Samuel 17:26: *"Who is this uncircumcised*

Philistine that he should defy the armies of the living God?" God wants to rise up and do miracles for the glory of his Name.

6. **Use testimonies of answered prayer and God's provision to encourage the people.** Testimonies build faith and spur them to action, showing them how God has used people in similar situations to do great things.

[18] I also told them about the gracious hand of my God on me and what the king had said to me. They replied, "Let us start rebuilding (AMP: *rise up and rebuild").* So they began (AMP: *strengthened their hands for this good work;* Message: *They said, "We're with you. Let's get started." They rolled up their sleeves, ready for the good work.)*

7. **Get going!** Enough with meetings and endless talk! It's time to do something - in the Lord's time and in his way, of course. How we need this attitude in the church! What a shame that it's the leaders who often stand in the way!

- Many just need a little encouragement. They were living in the middle of ruins – and no one did anything. They were overwhelmed.

- Talk is cheap. TV's full of it. But too often it never leads to action; to putting the Word into practice.

- They were disheartened, but when an anointed man like Nehemiah brings a true word from God, their hands were strengthened.

- The leaders and the people were in agreement: "Let's get going!"

- We can use pressure and guilt, but if the people aren't motivated, nothing will happen. When we follow Nehemiah's example they'll roll up their sleeves and get busy.

[19] But when Sanballat the Horonite, Tobiah the Ammonite official and Geshem the Arab heard about it, they mocked and ridiculed us. "What is this you are doing?" they asked. "Are you rebelling against the king?"

8. As always, **you can count on opposition** from the enemy every step of the way.

- They mock you.
- They ridicule you.
- They question your motives.
- They sow fear and doubt in your heart with their threats.

Is someone mocking you or your church? Are they ridiculing you? Is there fear or doubt you need to renounce?

20 *I answered them by saying, "The God of heaven will give us success. We his servants will start rebuilding, but as for you, you have no share in Jerusalem or any claim or historic right to it."*

9. **Keep going.** Don't stop for anything. Don't be moved from what God has called you to do. Stand firm on his Word.

- Your confidence is in God, so keep your eyes on him. It's God's work, his battle, and his victory. They're his servants – and they're going to obey their Master.

- Nehemiah tells the enemies exactly who they are – unbelievers who have no part in the Lord's work or the holy city. Of course they're not going to understand what he's doing!

- Come what may, despite everything that comes against them, they're going to get up and build. If they die in the process, so be it. No matter how hard the enemy tries to stop us, we must keep building the Kingdom of God.

10. **Resist the temptation to go it alone.** It's hard to deal with people. We've all been wounded and betrayed. Everybody has some dysfunction! People will disappoint you. It often looks easier to forget about them and just do it yourself. Or, like a man in a troubled marriage looking for a new wife, look for a new church or better

group of people to work with. That new church will have its own problems! You may initially have better results by yourself. It may seem to happen faster. But eventually the result will always be less. You need others. God could do just fine governing the universe all by himself, but he's chosen to share the job with us. Look at the headaches we've given him! A big part of your growth will come from learning how to work with people.

In many places today the church is in ruins. Walls of protection against the enemy have been broken down. It's a joke in the world's eyes. There's a lot of talk, but little action. We need men like Nehemiah. Are you available?

Chapter 4

Motivating the People
Nehemiah 3

You've managed to convince everyone the job needs to be done. Now your management and delegation skills will be put to the test. If you're a perfectionist or insist on doing most of the work yourself, the task will probably never get done – and you'll burn yourself out in the process.

¹Eliashib the high priest and his fellow priests went to work and rebuilt the Sheep Gate. They dedicated it and set its doors in place, building as far as the Tower of the Hundred, which they dedicated, and as far as the Tower of Hananel. ² The men of Jericho built the adjoining section, and Zakkur son of Imri built next to them.

The people are motivated and ready to work. All they need is someone to guide them, someone with an action plan. Many leaders fail here. They don't know how to manage people. They haven't prepared a plan. They've prayed and asked God to raise up workers – but when he answers and the people are ready to go, there's nothing for them to do. And we waste a great opportunity.

Here's the model Nehemiah successfully followed to finish the job:

1. He assigned a gate or portion of the wall to a family or group. Here it's the priests and men of Jericho. Look for people with similar backgrounds, the same language, from the same town; people who already have a natural connection. They understand the culture. God willing, there will be less conflict. It will be easier to get the work done.

2. When we divide up the task it becomes manageable. Looking at the whole wall it's easy to feel overwhelmed, but when you're given one gate to work on it becomes doable. And when you see the gate finished you feel like you've done something valuable. You've done your part. Maybe that's why the priests, when they finished the Sheep Gate, kept going on a section of the wall. Instead of saying "we're going to paint the church", or "let's evangelize the city", assign each family a room in the church to paint, or a block in the city for a small group to evangelize.

3. There will be healthy competition between the groups to finish and do a good job. Men are competitive by nature. Make the work a game. Find something to compliment and be free to

recognize a job done well. It's not to feed their pride; we need appropriate recognition. Too often it's missing in the church.

Can you see a big potential problem?

Few of them had experience building walls. Each family would probably do their section of the wall differently – and possibly not too well. The wall wouldn't be perfect or uniform. That's okay! We tend to put unrealistic expectations on the church and our families! The people get discouraged, feeling they can never measure up to our standards, so they don't do anything! It's more important for everyone to be working than to have a perfect wall.

Jesus said children are the most important in the kingdom of God. Remember your kids? How they wanted to help you – but didn't do things according to your adult expectations? And they left discouraged, maybe crying, with the feeling they'd never be good enough to please their dad. Next time they didn't want to help you. The work might not measure up to the world's standards – or yours - but God may be very pleased with it. The job is to build a wall – not to do it perfectly. Solomon's temple was beautiful – and it got knocked down.

Continuing the Work

The chapter names different families and their part in the task. Everyone was working - it wasn't optional. Nehemiah notes several things of interest:

*⁵ The next section was repaired by the men of Tekoa, but **their nobles would not put their shoulders to the work under their supervisors.***

This may have been the only time that some – here it was the nobles – rebelled and refused to work. It's impressive that everyone else respected Nehemiah's authority and accepted their assigned task. Often there's someone – usually someone who thinks they're important – who doesn't want to get with the program. They may feel they're better than their supervisors. Don't worry about it. Keep going with everyone else. Don't cater to them. When they see everyone working and the wall going up, they'll be convicted of their sin.

*¹² Shallum son of Hallohesh, ruler of a half-district of Jerusalem, repaired the next section **with the help of his daughters.***

Maybe Shallum didn't have any sons, but it's significant for that time that the girls were also working. They may not be professionals, but include everyone in the Lord's work, even the elderly and handicapped.

*²⁰ Next to him, Baruch son of Zabbai **zealously** repaired another section, from the angle to the entrance of the house of Eliashib the high priest.*

Wouldn't it be great if everyone did their work zealously? Spanish versions say *with enthusiasm*. We're all different. In every group there'll be some who aren't into it, and others who are enthusiastic. The leader's job is to direct that zeal and enthusiasm to motivate the whole group, not to put the others down and make the zealous brother seem better. The wise leader knows how to make that enthusiasm contagious, and at the same time make sure the grumbling and discouragement doesn't spread, because that can happen very easily. Leaders may quench zeal because they feel threatened by it, or be concerned that the enthusiastic youngsters aren't doing things quite the way they would. Don't do it. That zeal and enthusiasm are necessary to get the job done.

It would be interesting to know what made Baruch's zeal so noticeable. Hopefully you haven't lost your zeal and enthusiasm. We want to encourage that zeal in the whole church!

*²³ Beyond them, Benjamin and Hasshub made repairs **in front of their house**; and next to them, Azariah son of Maaseiah, the son of Ananiah, made repairs **beside his house**.*

People tend to be more interested in repairing something close to their homes. We get excited about a project in our neighborhood, or something that will affect our own family.

Nehemiah had a huge task that would be impossible if the people refused to do their part. All his excellent preparation could have been useless. I've seen a lot of pastors who do most of the work in the church. They arrange the chairs, clean the building, make copies, and direct most of the services. It shouldn't be that way. We want to teach people to take responsibility for their church, their home, and their life. We want mature people, ready to work.

There's no shortage of great visions or people who've heard from the Lord. They may raise money for their work. But there are few who really know how to mobilize people to do the job. We have much to learn from Nehemiah.

Chapter 5

Fight for Your Family
Nehemiah 4

If you're serving the Lord there will be battles. Surprised? Did someone tell you when you accepted Christ that the battles would end? That if you did everything right and were walking in the Spirit there'd be constant victory? Sorry. I hate to tell you this, but there are going to be battles for the rest of your life. Are you tired of fighting? Do you feel like giving up? What's the alternative? Seriously. Suicide? Serving Satan?

When Jerusalem was in ruins and the people were doing nothing, Sanballat didn't bother them. But when they started rebuilding the walls, all hell broke loose. Sanballat and Tobiah were true thorns in Nehemiah's flesh who just wouldn't give up. Do you have a Sanballat? A thorn that's constantly bothering you? Can you believe God allows it and is using it to teach you many things? You may end up fighting the same battle over and over again. It's in the battle we really seek God and learn how to serve him.

¹When Sanballat heard that we were rebuilding the wall, he became angry and was greatly incensed. He ridiculed the Jews, ² and in the presence of his associates and the army of Samaria, he said, "What are those feeble Jews doing? Will they restore their wall? Will they offer sacrifices? Will they finish in a day? Can they bring the stones back to life from those heaps of rubble—burned as they are?"

³ Tobiah the Ammonite, who was at his side, said, "What they are building—even a fox climbing up on it would break down their wall of stones!"

The first stage of the enemy's attacks

The battle starts with your mind, with words that come as fiery darts from the evil one and wound your spirit. They hurt worse when the enemy uses someone close to you, like your wife, your boss, or a good friend. They put down what you're doing to the point you question if it's worthwhile. They ridicule your ethnic background, language, or faith, destroying your self-esteem and making you feel inferior. They make fun of you and spread lies about you. Today they'd be on Facebook, the internet, or TV telling everyone what a joke you are. They do everything possible to discourage you. Discouragement is a favorite tool of the devil. It does not come from God.

Are you faithfully serving Christ – and feeling so discouraged you're ready to give up? Rebuke the enemy and don't listen to him! Use your shield of faith to extinguish the fiery darts of the evil one! And seek the Lord!

Responding to the attack

Nehemiah, along with the people, responded to these attacks with prayer:

4 Hear us, our God, for we are despised. Turn their insults back on their own heads. Give them over as plunder in a land of captivity. 5 Do not cover up their guilt or blot out their sins from your sight, for they have thrown insults in the face of the builders.

They recognized it as a spiritual battle and fought on a spiritual level. Don't get into a war of words with Sanballat. Don't try to defend yourself. Call out to God. Nehemiah asked God to avenge them, something we often see in David's prayers, although it doesn't exactly reflect the love for our enemies that Jesus taught. What's essential is to call out to God and commit your situation to him. Let him deal with the people as he will, and keep going with the work. Don't stop for anything:

6 So we rebuilt the wall till all of it reached half its height, for the people worked with all their heart.

They're moving right along! The wall's already halfway up! And despite the opposition, under Nehemiah's capable leadership they're working with all their heart. But the enemy doesn't give up. He comes back with even more ferocious attacks.

⁷ But when Sanballat, Tobiah, the Arabs, the Ammonites and the people of Ashdod heard that the repairs to Jerusalem's walls had gone ahead and that the gaps were being closed, they were very angry. ⁸ They all plotted together to come and fight against Jerusalem and stir up trouble against it.

The next level of attack

Now they've ganged up with others and are plotting an attack on the city. At first Satan plays with your mind and comes against you with words. When that doesn't stop you, he'll change his tactics and attack physically. He'll stir up trouble in your family and your church or ministry.

The enemy gets really angry when he sees the gaps being closed. It may be areas where we've let things go, let down our defenses, or allowed sin to come in. The gaps give him access to your life, family, and church.

⁹ But we prayed to our God and posted a guard day and night to meet this threat.

Their faith and trust in God remain strong, and once again they come together in prayer. But they're no fools. I know Jesus said to turn the other cheek, but there are times when it's okay to take action, like putting new locks on the church building or removing internet access from your house. They post a twenty-four hour guard and amp up their vigilance. Analyze the threat and pray about how best to respond. Prepare yourself with God's armor and spiritual weapons.

Despite these steps, the enemy scores a victory:

10 Meanwhile, the people in Judah said, "The strength of the laborers is giving out, and there is so much rubble that we cannot rebuild the wall."

When the burden bearers burn out

The anxiety, heavy work, and constant attacks are taking their toll. They're worn out. The word for laborers actually means "burden bearers." In each church there are burden bearers who do most of the work. When their strength starts giving out you know you're in trouble. What happened here?

There was too much rubble - garbage from past defeats - that's getting in the way of moving ahead. If possible, clean out the rubble from the past before trying to rebuild your life or your church. The garbage just serves as a distraction and something the enemy can use to discourage you.

They're ready to give up. The task seems too big and the opposition too great. They begin to feel it's impossible. Most of us have been there. In the flesh, what you're facing is overwhelming. This is a crucial turning point. Many leave the wall half built, which is useless. After everything Nehemiah has done, it's easy to lose the battle right here.

[11] Also our enemies said, "Before they know it or see us, we will be right there among them and will kill them and put an end to the work."

The devil's ultimate objective

Jesus said the devil came to steal, kill, and destroy. When the enemy sees you worn down and discouraged he intensifies his attacks. Now it's not just a battle of words and mind games. It doesn't even stop with an attack on the city and their work. He wants to kill them. And that is what Satan wants to do with you: kill you. That's one sure way to stop God's work.

The devil loves sneak attacks. He waits until you're tired and your defenses are down, and jumps you. Open your eyes! Wake up! Many Christians are asleep and unaware of the devil's schemes. The enemy is in their midst without them knowing it, and suddenly their marriage is ruined or the church split.

Is it possible Satan has snuck into your family or church? Is he ready to pounce on you right now to kill you? Are you looking death in the face? Is he about to shut down the ministry?

12 Then the Jews who lived near them came and told us ten times over, "Wherever you turn, they will attack us."

Now the enemy's using believers to discourage them. They're scared, with no faith or vision. All they can see is the enemy. They're already defeated, and their constant warnings and crying can spread like cancer. It would be very easy for Nehemiah to say "enough" and go back to the king's palace in Babylon. The battle is just too much. How is he going to handle it?

13 Therefore I stationed some of the people behind the lowest points of the wall at the exposed places, posting them by families, with their swords, spears and bows. 14 After I looked things over, I stood up and said to the nobles, the officials and the rest of the people, "Don't be afraid of them. Remember the Lord, who is great and awesome, and fight for your families, your sons and your daughters, your wives and your homes."

Nehemiah doesn't miss a beat. He addresses the threat and organizes the people to defend themselves. When the battle is this intense, it becomes a full-time job. Forget about movies, vacation, or even rest. They're in a life or death struggle. Their survival is in question. Will they end up with a secure city? Or spend their lives in fear, taunted by the enemy, and probably serving him? Very likely they'll die and lose everything.

The critical importance of godly leadership

Nehemiah carefully looks things over, analyzing the situation. He goes to God, waiting for a word from the Lord, and his plan. Then he calls the people - your family, or the church - together.

Just as with Moses, it's up to one man to save the day. This is no time for the man of God to get discouraged and question his faith. As the head of your house, your family needs you. If you're a pastor, your church needs you. You may need to seek God like never before, but then get up and bring them God's Word. Tell God – and possibly a brother you really trust –your doubts and fears, but this is not the time to be transparent about your weaknesses. There are three essential responses:

1. Don't be afraid of them. Fear destroys faith. If fear overwhelms you, you've already lost the battle.

2. Remember the Lord! The God of the universe. The one in total control. Get your eyes on him and off your situation. Worship him. Read his Word. Remind yourself of his power and the great things he's done for his people. Remember his words to Joshua: *No one will be able to withstand you*.

3.   Finally, the bottom line: Fight for your family. If nothing else motivates you, think about your parents and brothers and sisters. Fight for your home. For that woman you love so much. For that beautiful little girl, and for your son. Get up like a man. Don't let Satan have your kids. Don't give in to the devil's plans for that divorce. I've known too many weak men who just sit and watch Satan destroy their families, feeling helpless. They never get serious about fighting in prayer and in the Spirit. Get up! Speak God's Word to them! Keep on going!

15 When our enemies heard that we were aware of their plot and that God had frustrated it, we all returned to the wall, each to our own work. 16 From that day on, half of my men did the work, while the other half were equipped with spears, shields, bows and armor. The officers posted themselves behind all the people of Judah 17 who were building the wall. Those who carried materials did their work with one hand and held a weapon in the other, 18 and each of the builders wore his sword at his side as he worked. But the man who sounded the trumpet stayed with me.

19 Then I said to the nobles, the officials and the rest of the people, "The work is extensive and spread out, and we are widely separated from each other along the wall. 20 Wherever you hear the sound of the trumpet, join us there. Our God will fight for us!"

21 So we continued the work with half the men holding spears, from the first light of dawn till the stars came out. 22 At that time I also said to the people, "Have every man and his helper stay inside Jerusalem at night, so they can serve us as guards by night and as workers by day." 23 Neither I nor my brothers nor my men nor the guards with me took off our clothes; each had his weapon, even when he went for water.

He did it! When a man does what Nehemiah did here, we need to celebrate! God has another victory!

The battle's not over. There's still lots to do. But the enemy recognizes his defeat and backs off. He's been exposed. Nehemiah and the people know what he's up to. He's lost his advantage of surprise and deceit. Even the enemy can see God's hand. Somehow they knew it was God who frustrated their plot, and they're too smart to fight with him.

We may want to take a rest, but when the battle's over it's important to get back to the work God's given us. They all return to their jobs. Everyone has a task assigned to them. It's a lot of work with practically no rest. In fact, Nehemiah makes things far more demanding:

- They can't stop working or let down their guard. While half the people work, the others are armed, defending the wall.

- The leaders have the peoples' backs. They were posted behind them to make sure everything was okay. Nehemiah's great, but he can't do it all himself. He needs the leaders to be awake and watchful. Whenever they detect a problem, discouragement, or grumbling, they move on it quickly to keep it from spreading. Everyone was important.

- Communication is essential, so an alarm system was established. When a threat was detected, the trumpet would sound and everyone would respond. They're one people, and unity was critical. Today we might use Twitter, Facebook, texts, or the phone. No one should be alone, beat up by the enemy. If a member of your family or church is under attack, the believers need to join together to do whatever is necessary to help them.

- We can make the best arrangements, but our trust is in God. Nehemiah knew God was fighting for them, and that should serve as tremendous encouragement.

- They worked the entire day – and never even took their clothes off! They had to be ready night or day. They've seen the enemy's power and determination. This is no time to rest. The daily routine gets put aside. This isn't about a half hour of prayer and that should do it; life continues as always. No, if your son is on drugs and your wife's with another man, if the devil's coming against you hard, you've got to focus on the battle. It's going to take everything you've got.

Can you see how a battle forces you to give one hundred percent to the Lord? How it forces us to work together? Does God possibly allow these battles because they teach us so much? If they didn't work together and cover each other's back, they wouldn't make it. Could it be we lose people in the church because we still haven't learned this simple lesson? We're lazy, complacent, and caught up with our own pleasure.

My brother, this is not a game. I'm serious. Satan wants you dead. He wants to destroy your family and your church. You may be the Nehemiah God raises up as his instrument to save them. Don't give up. Keep fighting. Let's fight together. Fight for your family. Nobody can withstand us.

Chapter 6

Dealing With Injustice
Nehemiah 5

Nehemiah finally silenced his enemies. The attacks started with verbal onslaughts, proceeded to threats against the work, and finished with attempts to kill them. But God honored Nehemiah's faith and steadfastness, fought the battles, and protected his people. Work on the wall is progressing, though it requires extraordinary measures.

The enemy's next tactic: Internal strife

Unfortunately, the battle's not over. We've seen the importance of unity in the face of relentless opposition. You can imagine the stress on people who barely have a chance to sleep, fearing a surprise attack at any moment. The enemy sees their weakness and adopts a new strategy: creating internal strife.

¹Now the men and their wives raised a great outcry against their fellow Jews. ² Some were saying, "We and our sons and daughters are numerous; in order for us to eat and stay alive, we must get grain."

41

³ Others were saying, "We are mortgaging our fields, our vineyards and our homes to get grain during the famine."

⁴ Still others were saying, "We have had to borrow money to pay the king's tax on our fields and vineyards. ⁵Although we are of the same flesh and blood as our fellow Jews and though our children are as good as theirs, yet we have to subject our sons and daughters to slavery. Some of our daughters have already been enslaved, but we are powerless, because our fields and our vineyards belong to others."

Apparently this had been going on for some time and Nehemiah wasn't aware of it. That's understandable. He certainly had his hands full. But long-simmering frustrations, fueled by glaring economic inequality and exploitation, are finally expressed in a great outcry. It's particularly troubling that the perpetrators are fellow Jews.

Some were feasting while others were starving. A famine aggravated an already bad situation and resulted in widespread hunger. There was grain - but those who had it were charging exorbitant prices, forcing the poor to mortgage everything they owned. At least they had property to mortgage! Many poor people don't even have that. The poor also had to borrow money to pay taxes to the king. Some sort of tax relief was necessary.

With no apparent alternative, in desperation they sold their children to stay alive. Slavery became common.

Poverty creates powerlessness. The poor lose their voice and get caught in a vicious cycle that's hard to escape. Up to now they had no advocate. Without some intervention Judah would become a society of haves and have-nots. This kind of inequality – among believers - raises perplexing questions: Don't our children deserve good schools? Why can't they have the same opportunities to prepare for a career? Is it really true that all men are created equal? And if so, how come those who espouse that ideal don't seem to practice it?

The enemy exploits these legitimate complaints to bring division and stop God's work. Churches split over much less! If you're married, I'm sure you know how a minor issue can become major under the right circumstances. What kind of divide and conquer tactics have you seen Satan use in marriages? In the church? Are there legitimate complaints simmering under the surface in your church or home?

Underlying these abuses is the sinful human tendency to seek the upper hand and take advantage of others; to look out for number one. In the process we ignore the most important commands about love and mercy and justice.

[6] When I heard their outcry and these charges, I was very angry.

They finally found a defender in Nehemiah, who was filled with righteous anger. Do you get angry about injustice? Do you get angry when you see divisions and inequality in the church? Have you bothered to listen to the outcry? It's easy to comfortably distance ourselves from *their* problems. Not all anger is bad! But it should energize you to take constructive action.

[7] I pondered them in my mind and then accused the nobles and officials. I told them, "You are charging your own people interest!" So I called together a large meeting to deal with them [8] and said: "As far as possible, we have bought back our fellow Jews who were sold to the Gentiles. Now you are selling your own people, only for them to be sold back to us!"

Responding to internal conflicts in the church

Jesus said *"Blessed are the peacemakers."* We need peacemakers today. Pastors who are great preachers often are at a loss to deal with conflict in the church. Men who manage their office well may withdraw at home, clueless on how to resolve the conflicts. Nehemiah was one of those unusual multi-talented men. How does he deal with this issue?

There was no knee-jerk reaction. We usually get in trouble when we angrily lash out. He pondered what he heard, perhaps verifying the reports. That done, he wasn't afraid to confront those responsible. Too many pastors back down before the elders, deacons, or wealthy donors. Too many husbands don't want to be bothered with family problems. Nehemiah did what was politically risky. It's never easy, but don't just ignore the issues and hope they go away. They usually don't. What often does go away is a sizable part of your congregation, or your wife. Stand up for what you know is right!

Next, he challenged a common business practice: charging interest on loans. There had been a "buy-back program" to free indentured Jews from Gentile owners. But instead of the wealthy helping them get established, they hypocritically substituted another kind of slavery! We need to be careful of following the world system in the church. What would the economic impact be if Christians started loaning each other money interest-free? Jesus said not to worry about getting paid back (Matthew 5:42)! He'll take care of you! Nehemiah didn't work out some back-room deal. It's riskier and requires more strength, but he called everyone together in a large meeting. As we've seen before, the man had tremendous authority, and he used it wisely.

8They kept quiet, because they could find nothing to say.

9 So I continued, "What you are doing is not right. Shouldn't you walk in the fear of our God to avoid the reproach of our Gentile enemies? [10] I and my brothers and my men are also lending the people money and grain. But let us stop charging interest! [11] Give back to them immediately their fields, vineyards, olive groves and houses, and also the interest you are charging them—one percent of the money, grain, new wine and olive oil."

What Nehemiah proposes is bold – and costly. Too often no one is willing to do the hard work to set things right. If you're a pastor, it falls on you. If you're a husband, it's your responsibility. The unity of your church and home is priority.

There are gray areas, but when it's black and white, we're obligated to stand up for what's right and condemn what's wrong. The powerful are clearly in the wrong here. They lack any fear of God and have forgotten they have to answer to their Creator for the treatment of their fellow man. Is there a situation at work, at church, or at home where you need to take the risk and say "What you're doing is wrong?" Are you walking in the fear of the Lord?

They're giving a bad testimony to their gentile enemies, and they don't care. They need to repent; stop what they're doing and make things right. Give back what was mortgaged and refund the interest paid – even though it was only one percent! Most of us would be thrilled if we could get such a deal! But in the family of

God it's wrong for one to prosper at others' expense. When believers act like the world it makes God look bad. What a disgrace that the church is often a laughing stock. We are to walk blamelessly, so people will see Jesus in us, be drawn to him, and glorify him. What kind of testimony are you giving? Are you doing something that deep down you know is wrong? Even though it may be painful, how can you make it right? How do you think people around you would respond if you challenged them like this?

12 "We will give it back," they said. "And we will not demand anything more from them. We will do as you say."

Then I summoned the priests and made the nobles and officials take an oath to do what they had promised. 13 I also shook out the folds of my robe and said, "In this way may God shake out of their house and possessions anyone who does not keep this promise. So may such a person be shaken out and emptied!"

It's hard to argue with someone who tells the truth and provides a righteous way to remedy the situation. They know they're wrong, and they know Nehemiah's not going to let them get away with it. There's a huge difference between a timid, weak, challenge, and someone who boldly speaks with God's authority. Nehemiah had spoken with that authority to Sanballat and Tobiah. He could speak words of judgment that weren't just empty threats. The Spirit of God is backing him up. We need righteous leaders with that authority in our churches and government!

An amazing response

13At this the whole assembly said, "Amen," and praised the Lord. And the people did as they had promised.

Nehemiah makes them give up bunches of money and rebukes them in front of everyone – and they end up praising the Lord?! And they do as they promised? This is true repentance! This is the spirit of revival! When God is moving, when a man of God finally stands up and confronts injustice with divine authority, a release takes place. I've heard many prisoners say: "I'm glad I got caught and am doing this time, because I knew what I was doing was wrong, but I didn't know how to get out of it." Does that mean there's no pain involved? Of course not, but Nehemiah gave them a way out. Now the Spirit is free to move, and God receives the praise.

Getting right with God isn't just about going to church, tithing, and reading your Bible. It has a whole lot to do with how you run your business, respond to injustice, and treat others. Nehemiah had no need to repent. He could have smugly sat back and looked down on the wrongdoers, or ignored it, taking solace in the thought that he was right with God. But that's not enough.

You're obligated to speak up for what's right. Nehemiah could do that because he was blameless.

How we need people like Nehemiah today! As a result of his wise response, a potentially debilitating division is healed. Once again the enemy is foiled. But Nehemiah wasn't done yet. He didn't just respond to the problem - he moved pro-actively to foster understanding and unity. It's easy to sit back and relax once the immediate crisis is addressed. Far better to have the vision to make a lasting change to prevent future problems.

[14] Moreover, from the twentieth year of King Artaxerxes, when I was appointed to be their governor in the land of Judah, until his thirty-second year—twelve years— neither I nor my brothers ate the food allotted to the governor. [15]But the earlier governors—those preceding me—placed a heavy burden on the people and took forty shekels of silver from them in addition to food and wine. Their assistants also lorded it over the people. But out of reverence for God I did not act like that. [16] Instead, I devoted myself to the work on this wall. All my men were assembled there for the work; we did not acquire any land.

[17]Furthermore, a hundred and fifty Jews and officials ate at my table, as well as those who came to us from the surrounding nations. [18] Each day one ox, six choice sheep and some poultry were prepared for me, and every ten days an abundant supply of wine of all kinds. In spite of

all this, I never demanded the food allotted to the governor, because the demands were heavy on these people.

Nehemiah leads the way in showing true love

Nehemiah wasn't just an authoritarian enforcer. He led by example, and he was consistent. This wasn't a passing show of piety. For twelve years he gave the same example. As governor, he was given a special allotment of food. Many pastors today would jump on that as "God's blessing" which they deserve. They're only too ready to take advantage of any benefit clergy may receive. Nehemiah didn't. He refused to live better than his brothers. He must have had a pretty large house and kitchen, but it was for the people! At least 150 ate with him every day – at his expense. What a tremendous way to build relationships! It's not wrong to have a large house and ample resources! It's what you do with it! Is it right for believers to have huge houses with empty bedrooms when there are Christian families living in homeless shelters across town?

Nehemiah was well aware of the burdens on the people and refused to make them any heavier. He broke a long-standing tradition. Previous governors heavily taxed those who couldn't afford it. What a tragedy when high-living pastors pressure their people to give more, and encourage special "love offerings" so they can go on cruises or "mission trips." Nehemiah wasn't after their money. Instead of lording it over them, hundreds of years before Christ he demonstrated the kind of leadership Jesus commanded: *"The kings of the Gentiles lord it over them; and those who exercise authority over them call themselves Benefactors. But you are not to be like that. Instead, the greatest among you should be like the youngest, and the one who rules like the one who serves."* (Luke 22:25-26) Nehemiah worked shoulder to shoulder with the people. He wasn't afraid to get his hands dirty. He identified with them, and made sure the other leaders did the same.

He did all this out of reverence for God, or, more literally, out of the fear of God. He knew he was under God's authority and answerable to him. Far be it from him to take advantage of God's people!

[19] Remember me with favor, my God, for all I have done for these people.

None of this was easy. It wasn't popular and probably came at great personal expense. It would have been far easier to side with the rich and maintain the status quo, but he couldn't do that and stand before his God. He could have stayed in a comfortable palace in Babylon. He had nothing to gain from these headaches, but the love of God compelled him to act. He is seeking blessing - but not earthly, material blessing. He trusts God to reward him - if not in this life, then in eternity. Jesus said if we seek rewards in this life, that's all we'll receive (Matthew 6:2, 5). Far better to follow Nehemiah's example and wait for our heavenly reward! God remembers everything you've done for him and will reward it!

Chapter 7

Remember the Gates!
Nehemiah 6

Nehemiah handled one crisis after another with wisdom, grace, and strength. When conflicts among the believers threatened to stop the work, God gave him a bold solution, and they emerged from the trial even stronger.

That's how it should be in your life as well. There will always be problems. If things are great on the job, it will be something at home. And if your home is fine, it will be the church. But God brings us through, teaching and refining us, so we end up better than before. Trials no longer have to elicit despair, but excitement at yet another opportunity to see God do the impossible (see James 1:2-5). Life becomes better than a video game! It's real!

1Word came to Sanballat, Tobiah, Geshem the Arab and the rest of our enemies that I had rebuilt the wall and not a gap was left in it—though up to that time I had not set the doors in the gates.

They've made amazing progress! The wall is rebuilt. All the gaps are closed. They only have to set the doors in the gates. Nehemiah obviously didn't do all the work, but as the one in charge he's been the focus of attack, and he says *I* rebuilt it. To his enemies, it's his work. When you're in leadership there's a legitimate sense of ownership over what you've accomplished, but Nehemiah can't savor his victory for long. If he was tempted with pride, these constant battles kept him humble. Just when things were going well, our old friends Sanballat and Tobiah show up again, along with the whole gang. With the wall complete, the enemy knows he has to move fast. Soon it will be too late. He's got to do whatever he can to stop those doors from being hung.

The importance of gates

We're in the last days. The wall is built and we're closing the gaps. By God's grace, the bride is almost ready. Satan is desperate, unleashing all his demons to deceive and destroy as many Christians as possible. And it's at the gates that we're vulnerable. The wall may be strong, but the devil can come in like a flood through just one open gate.

You've worked hard to build a solid wall of obedience to the Word of God. You've searched out all the gaps and closed them - gaps where the enemy attacked and almost destroyed you in the past. Things like besetting sins, addictions, generational curses, sexual or physical abuse, and old wounds. If you haven't closed those gaps, gates will do no good. First you have to repair the broken down parts of your life. By God's grace you can receive healing and rebuild the walls. Then you can think about the gates in your life and home.

Unfortunately, many people, families, and churches have great walls – but leave the doors wide open. The devil doesn't have to attack you - he simply walks through the door. What are some of those doors? The internet, TV, radio, friendships, sins, and agreements we've made with the enemy.

When the doors are closed

Even with all the doors closed, the devil will still look for a way to destroy you. Here he tries to get Nehemiah outside the safety of the walled city, away from the community of faith.

2 Sanballat and Geshem sent me this message: "Come, let us meet together in one of the villages on the plain of Ono." But they were scheming to harm me.

Praise the Lord! People who had been against you are finally inviting you over! They recognize Nehemiah's importance and want to get to know him! Or do they? Don't be naïve. God can do a miracle and change someone's heart, but be careful! The devil is very shrewd. He's a liar and deceiver. Look below the surface for the motives. Nehemiah doesn't trust them. He can spot a wolf in sheep's clothing. Never trust the devil!

They're trying to get him out of his element. Only Nehemiah is invited. Spanish translations communicate a sense of urgency ("we *have* to meet"). It's all very suspicious. If someone wants to meet with you, why can't they come to your house? Or your office? Why don't they want your wife or the assistant pastor there? Why the rush now, after all this time? Why the sudden change of heart?

³ So I sent messengers to them with this reply: "I am carrying on a great project and cannot go down. Why should the work stop while I leave it and go down to you?"

Keep your priorities straight and be a man of your word

I've seen pastors offend well-meaning people of other religions or different beliefs, insulting them and almost cursing them. That's not necessary. Nehemiah makes a simple, firm, response: "I'm busy with something very important. The Lord's work has priority. I can't go." He closes the door. Many need to learn how to firmly and graciously say "no". Be careful of saying you'll go, out of fear and a desire to avoid confrontation, when you have no intention of going. Be a man of your word. To say you'll do something and then not do it is lying and a bad testimony, even though it's common in many cultures.

Nehemiah communicates the importance of what he's doing. He has priorities, and he can't leave something so critical to waste his time. Many pastors don't know how to make and keep priorities. They suffer from what is called the "tyranny of the urgent," and leave a trail of unfinished projects. They feel obligated to answer every call or text. They're always running around and not getting much done. We need the Holy Spirit to show us how to make wise use of the time God gives us.

[4] Four times they sent me the same message, and each time I gave them the same answer.

Stand firm!

The world knows how to wear you down. Especially young people. You may be able to say no the first time a friend offers you a beer. Even the second time. But by the fourth time you may give in and take it, not wanting to offend him. Or it could be the temptation of pornography on the internet. The first time something uninvited shows up on your screen you can click it off. But when it shows up night after night you finally say, "Well, just once, for a few minutes." Or the guy pressuring his girlfriend... You know how it goes.

Nehemiah stood fast. He never changed his response. He didn't waste any time. When someone sees that you won't be moved, eventually they'll give up.

Same thing happens with Satan. When he sees one temptation isn't working, he'll try something else.

5 Then, the fifth time, Sanballat sent his aide to me with the same message, and in his hand was an unsealed letter 6in which was written: "It is reported among the nations—and Geshem says it is true—that you and the Jews are plotting to revolt, and therefore you are building the wall. Moreover, according to these reports you are about to become their king 7 and have even appointed prophets to make this proclamation about you in Jerusalem: 'There is a king in Judah!' Now this report will get back to the king; so come, let us meet together."

Threats and intimidation

The enemy's an expert at using fear! He may say: "I know something about you, and if you don't do what I want you to, I'm going to talk to your wife, or your pastor, or your boss." Here it was nothing but lies, but lies can still destroy you! And when there's a kernel of truth in the lie it can produce even more fear!

8 I sent him this reply: "Nothing like what you are saying is happening; you are just making it up out of your head."

Has the devil made things up to intimidate you? Does his condemnation get to you? Nehemiah doesn't fall into that trap. When you're walking blamelessly with God, don't be afraid of the devil's lies.

⁹ They were all trying to frighten us, thinking, "Their hands will get too weak for the work, and it will not be completed."

But I prayed, "Now strengthen my hands."

Have you experienced those kinds of attacks? Something puts intense fear in your heart. You feel like giving up. It's just not worth it. You can't seem to find the strength to keep going.

Cry out to God, like Nehemiah did! He prayed because he needed his hands strengthened! Their words were getting to him! But he didn't want to give the enemy any room. There's a way out of every temptation! Call on the Lord and he will help you!

¹⁰ One day I went to the house of Shemaiah son of Delaiah, the son of Mehetabel, who was shut in at his home. He said, "Let us meet in the house of God, inside the temple, and let us close the temple doors, because men are coming to kill you—by night they are coming to kill you."

¹¹ But I said, "Should a man like me run away? Or should someone like me go into the temple to save his life? I will not go!"

False prophets

This is an interesting twist! A "brother" has a word for Nehemiah. We don't know why he went to his house. Maybe Nehemiah expected some words of encouragement. Instead he gets alarming news: that very night the enemy is coming to kill him, but he can hide in the temple. Sounds good.

Are there times you just want to hide? Maybe in the church? When I worked in prisons, the chapel was a safe place where someone could hide. If they "got religion" usually no one would touch them. But Nehemiah was a man of remarkable courage. He won't use religion to save his life. He's no coward. He's always stood up to his enemies.

12 I realized that God had not sent him, but that he had prophesied against me because Tobiah and Sanballat had hired him. 13 He had been hired to intimidate me so that I would commit a sin by doing this, and then they would give me a bad name to discredit me.

How we need the Spirit's discernment! Be careful! There are many false prophets out there! Don't listen to everyone who comes with a "word from the Lord." There are many sent by the devil, not God.

Sanballat and Tobiah are desperate! They just can't get to Nehemiah! The wall's almost done! So they've hired a supposed prophet to do an inside job, intimidate him, and make him sin. They can't find any dirt on him, so they're trying to make up something to give him a bad name.

I suspect most Christians today would buy this story and hide in the temple, believing it's okay to save your life and be in church. Never underestimate the lengths the enemy will go to! Make sure you pray through everything you do and think carefully about the ramifications!

[14] Remember Tobiah and Sanballat, my God, because of what they have done; remember also the prophet Noadiah and how she and the rest of the prophets have been trying to intimidate me.

We don't know for sure, but it sounds like most of the prophets had been bought off by the enemy! What should Nehemiah do? Return the favor and speak badly about this prophetess? Expose the others? No! Don't descend to their level! Keep on with your work! Give your adversaries over to the Lord. Nehemiah leaves them in God's hands.

I find the continuing intensity of the battle in these chapters amazing. Unfortunately there seem to be few who are up to it. Few with the wisdom, discernment, and strength of Nehemiah. It hurts when the devil uses pastors and prophets to destroy you, but God knows everything. They'll pay. Keep doing what God has called you to do.

How's your wall? Is your life still in ruins? Nehemiah's given you a great example of how to start rebuilding. God wants to encourage you: despite all your problems you can have a new life. Are you tired of living in ruins? Are you ready to give your life to Jesus and get a new life?

Are there still gaps in your wall? You may feel anxious and afraid, full of inner turmoil, but don't know where it's coming from. To repair your wall you have to know where the enemy's getting in. Ask God to show you the gaps, and for the Holy Spirit to heal and repair them.

How are your gates? Are you missing some doors? Are there open doors or gates in your life, your home, or your church where Satan can still get in? How can you close them?

God is with you, just as he was with Nehemiah! Call on him and let him take charge of your battles.

Chapter 8

Politics
Nehemiah 6:15-19

Many visionaries start projects. Few finish them. Especially a project as ambitious and strongly opposed as rebuilding the walls of Jerusalem. Did you ever wonder if Nehemiah would actually pull it off? Sure, most of us already know the story, but it was a miracle, a great example of what one person anointed by the Holy Spirit can do.

15 So the wall was completed on the twenty-fifth of Elul, in fifty-two days.16 When all our enemies heard about this, all the surrounding nations were afraid and lost their self-confidence, because they realized that this work had been done with the help of our God.

It took them less than two months – fifty-two days – to finish the wall. Amazing! The enemies who used fear to intimidate and tear down Nehemiah and the workers were humbled, ashamed of all their lies and attacks. Their prideful self-confidence was replaced by fear. They saw God's hand. They'd lost the battle.

How many projects are there today which can only be done with God's help, so he's glorified? The truth is, with all our resources we can do a great deal without God. There's a lot done in the flesh. Do you think God has some walls he wants rebuilt today? Could a miracle hush our critics and put the fear of God in their hearts?

Not surprisingly, Nehemiah's problems didn't end with the completion of the wall.

17 Also, in those days the nobles of Judah were sending many letters to Tobiah, and replies from Tobiah kept coming to them. 18 For many in Judah were under oath to him, since he was son-in-law to Shekaniah son of Arah, and his son Jehohanan had married the daughter of Meshullam son of Berekiah. 19 Moreover, they kept reporting to me his good deeds and then telling him what I said. And Tobiah sent letters to intimidate me.

Although it was against God's law, the Jews had married into Tobiah's family. Oaths were even made to him, and alliances formed. God's very enemy was intimately connected to the Jewish community! Nehemiah is clearly an outsider, since he wouldn't compromise his beliefs. The nobles tolerated him, but their real allegiance was to Tobiah. They were two-faced spies, talking nice to Nehemiah but then telling Tobiah everything he said. Tobiah responded with intimidating letters. For him, Nehemiah was a competitor. He couldn't stop the construction of the walls, but he was winning the battle for the people's hearts.

There will always be politics and personal dynamics to navigate if you are to be successful. While acknowledging they exist, don't get pulled into them and compromise what God has called you to do. Satan will use them to try to divert your attention from what is truly important.

Guidance on handling politics

Here are a few possible scenarios:

- You (and hopefully your wife) may be the only believers in her family. They're suspicious of your faith and what you're trying to do to their daughter and grandchildren. Your wife is in a difficult place, torn between you, her family, and the Lord. You need godly wisdom and love to gain their confidence, support your wife, give a good testimony, and stay true to God. It's not easy!

- You may be called to pastor a church that's gone through a split or internal conflicts. Some still feel allegiance to the former pastor. Others expect you to step in and set everything right. There's all kinds of politics. Don't get caught up in it. There's still great potential for division. Be careful taking sides. You may hope the troublemakers leave, but you're the pastor of the whole church. Repentance and reconciliation is almost always better than separation. Remember, just as in marital conflicts, there are always two sides to the story.

- You may be promoted at your job, but some are jealous because they feel they should have gotten the promotion. Others are close friends with the former supervisor. Be careful. You're going to need everyone's support in your new position. Don't get involved in the politics and gossip common in many workplaces.

Intimidation

You may face intimidation in each one of these situations. It's an important theme in this chapter.

- In verse thirteen Sanballat and Tobiah paid a prophet to intimidate Nehemiah, with the goal of causing him to sin.

- In verse fourteen Nehemiah realized that several "prophets" were trying to intimidate him. The devil may use people in the church to intimidate you.

- Now, in verse nineteen, when Tobiah didn't succeed with the prophets, he sends letters to intimidate Nehemiah.

Intimidate means to frighten someone, especially in order to make them do what they want. The Hebrew word appears 332 times in the Old Testament, almost always translated fear, or afraid. Fear and intimidation come from Satan, and are among his favorite weapons. He wants to paralyze you, so you'll submit to him and he can control you. Intimidation causes discouragement, confusion, and frustration. You lose your perspective. Everything seems overwhelming. You end up hopeless.

Are you being intimidated right now? By whom? Are you tempted to sin as a result? How can you respond to intimidation?

- Don't pay too much attention to it.

- Focus on the Lord and do spiritual battle. God's perfect love casts out fear!

- Be polite with your adversaries, and recognize who's behind what they're doing

- Keep a close watch on your heart. Don't get caught up in sin yourself or lose sight of what God has called you to do.

- Intimidation often results in the fear of man. We don't want to be rejected or hurt. Renounce that fear as sin – and fear God.

Follow Nehemiah's example:

- Stand firm on the Word of God and the authority he's given you. Truth breaks the spirit of intimidation.

- Recognize you're in a battle. Put on your spiritual armor and get up and fight! The boldness and faith we've seen in Nehemiah defeat intimidation.

If you want to study intimidation further, there's an excellent book by John Bevere called *Breaking Intimidation*.

Chapter 9

The Next Steps
Nehemiah 7:1-5

Undeterred by his enemies, Nehemiah keeps right on going with the work.

¹After the wall had been rebuilt and I had set the doors in place, the gatekeepers, the musicians and the Levites were appointed. ² I put in charge of Jerusalem my brother Hanani, along with Hananiah the commander of the citadel, because he was a man of integrity and feared God more than most people do. ³ I said to them, "The gates of Jerusalem are not to be opened until the sun is hot. While the gatekeepers are still on duty, have them shut the doors and bar them. Also appoint residents of Jerusalem as guards, some at their posts and some near their own houses."

Raise up capable leaders

Now it's time to find capable people to manage and oversee what you started. You can't do it all alone. Chances are God will call you to another project.

Nehemiah knows he won't be there forever. From the start, keep your eyes open for potential leaders you can train to keep things going. That was Jesus' approach. More important than healing the sick or teaching the multitudes was his investment in twelve men who would establish the church. Who are you investing in? Are you always on the lookout for men with potential?

When you place someone in a position, make sure to give him clear instructions on what to do and exactly what your expectations are. Get his assurance that he understands that and knows how to do it before you let him loose. Too many people are given tasks in the church without the necessary orientation, training, oversight, and support.

Nehemiah looked for people who stood out from the crowd. These men had exceptional integrity and fear of the Lord. Those qualities demonstrate a sincerity and commitment to God. Notice they weren't:

- The most popular
- The best educated
- The richest
- The most experienced
- The most religious

Many times it's the person who praises God the loudest, prays impressively, or knows the Bible well who gets our attention. But that doesn't necessarily reveal what their heart is like. They could be a Pharisee.

The qualities I've sought in leaders are:

- A teachable spirit. You don't need the person who thinks they know everything.
- Humility and a servant's heart, with a record of service in the church. Be careful of the person overly eager to be in leadership.
- A good testimony. Not perfect, but free from obvious sin and with evidence of genuine repentance. Honest about their faults and quick to ask forgiveness from God and others.
- Sincere love for God, the church, and the unsaved.

Nehemiah *appointed* leaders. We tend to go with volunteers, or even elect leaders, but the biblical model is to call and appoint them. God calls, and we discern his call and set them into that position.

4 Now the city was large and spacious, but there were few people in it, and the houses had not yet been rebuilt. 5 So my God put it into my heart to assemble the nobles, the officials and the common people for registration by families. I found the genealogical record of those who had been the first to return.

After the walls, rebuild the city

Nehemiah was already thinking about the next step. He rebuilt the walls – now he needed people to populate the city and rebuild the houses. Nobody wants to live in ruins. If the city is to prosper it must be attractive. This was part of Jesus' mission (Isaiah 61:4) – and part of ours as well.

To do this will require everyone's involvement, including the nobles who are allied with his enemy. God put it in his heart to assemble the people, to gather them together. Many projects start by getting people together, overlooking their differences to focus on a common goal. Often you won't hear an audible voice or get a clear word, but God will put a desire in your heart. Pay attention to those desires - and discern which are from God.

Nehemiah was a master organizer. He starts the next phase of the work by putting things in order and registering the people. Many leaders lack that gift of administration. Is there something you need to organize in your life, your family, or your church? The work will go much better that way!

Chapter 10

Your Genealogy is Important!
Nehemiah 7:64

My parents had charts on our family heritage. One branch still gets together every summer from all over the country, but I was never interested. Now that's changed, and I'm finding out all kinds of interesting things on Ancestry.com. There's so much, I'm not sure how to process it all, or what it means to me today. I even found one man who was a "king of Jerusalem" during the Crusades!

If you've read much of the Bible you know that genealogy is important to God. Both the Old Testament and the Gospels have chapters full of who begat who. Sometimes we think it's a waste of time to read them, but God has them there for a purpose. Knowing their tribe of origin was very important to the Jews. Jesus needed to prove he was of the tribe of Judah.

Nehemiah had already found some records:

I found the genealogical record of those who had been the first to return. (Nehemiah 7:5)

Still, I was surprised when I ran across this verse:

These searched for their family records, but they could not find them and so were excluded from the priesthood as unclean. (Nehemiah 7:64)

To serve as a priest you needed proof you were a Levite. Apparently most of them, even in the trauma of the exile, had kept their family records. But these poor men couldn't find them, and they were excluded from the priesthood and considered unclean.

Have you ever searched for your family records? Do you have any? Do you know anything about your heritage? Your genealogy is important to God! He's given you a unique heritage! Thank him for it! Most of my family — parents, grandparents, aunts and uncles — are dead. Don't delay! Talk to your grandparents and other relatives. Record them talking about their families. Ask God to guide you as you search for your family records. He may have surprises and blessings waiting for you!

Chapter 11

Four Keys to Revival
Nehemiah 8

Do you long for revival? In your own life? In your church? Nehemiah was best known for rebuilding Jerusalem's walls, but God also used him to bring revival to the city.

¹ All the people came together as one in the square before the Water Gate. They told Ezra the teacher of the Law to bring out the Book of the Law of Moses, which the Lord had commanded for Israel. ² So on the first day of the seventh month Ezra the priest brought the Law before the assembly, which was made up of men and women and all who were able to understand. ³ He read it aloud from daybreak till noon as he faced the square before the Water Gate in the presence of the men, women and others who could understand. And all the people listened attentively to the Book of the Law.

First key to revival: Preaching the Word

If we want revival it will start with the Book. I'm increasingly troubled at the lack of biblical preaching in our churches. Sure, we use a verse here and there as proof texts to support what we're saying. But the sad truth is there's massive ignorance of the Bible among Christians today. That's odd, isn't it? We have more - and better – translations than ever before. We have the Bible on our smart phones, so we can read it anytime, anywhere. To say nothing of all the resources on the internet.

Before doing anything else they opened the Scriptures.

- *All* the people gathered - men, women, and any children old enough to understand what was read. They came together *as one*. Often only the most committed members (who already know the Bible) attend Bible studies. Revival comes when there's unity, a unity based on the Word. I've stepped into churches with serious divisions, but when you simply preach the Bible, God brings them together around the Word.

- *They told* Ezra to get the Bible. Pastors often beg people to come to a Bible study. But here there was hunger for the Word.

- There was a teacher to read and explain the Word. Do you have teachers in your church who are equipped to interpret and explain the Bible? In many places where the church is growing rapidly, pastors are pushed into leadership with very little Bible knowledge. I don't believe seminary should be a requirement for ministry, but there's an alarming increase in pastors with virtually no biblical training. That leaves us open to all kinds of weird interpretations and false doctrine. Often the people aren't excited about hearing the Word because the pastor doesn't know how to present it. Instead he relies on stories, jokes, personal experience, and preaching he knows will get an emotional response.

- At first Ezra was simply *reading* the Word. Of course they didn't have Bibles. But the fact that our shelves are full of Bibles and we have several translations on our IPhones doesn't mean we're reading it. Do you have Bible reading in your church? In the Catholic church and some liturgical Protestant churches they read from the Old and New Testaments and the Gospels every week. How is it that churches supposedly more committed to the Bible don't even read it in their services? Is it because we think nobody would be interested? Or they'd be bored and go somewhere that's more exciting?

- They all *listened attentively* to the Word. Something's wrong if we're reading the Bible and people are texting, talking, or sleeping. If the Spirit of God is dwelling in them, there should be an excitement about hearing the Word.

7 The Levites —Jeshua, Bani, Sherebiah, Jamin, Akkub, Shabbethai, Hodiah, Maaseiah, Kelita, Azariah, Jozabad, Hanan and Pelaiah—instructed the people in the Law while the people were standing there. 8 They read from the Book of the Law of God, making it clear and giving the meaning so that the people understood what was being read.

There was a whole group of men equipped to teach the Scripture. That's interesting. They'd just gotten back from captivity and there were no established schools, but they managed to train these men to minister the Word. Does your church train people to teach the Bible?

They weren't giving their opinions or pop psychology. They did the three things which we also should do with the Word:

- They instructed the people. They taught the context and historical background; whatever was needed to make the Word come alive.

- They made it clear. Many people still find the Bible confusing. We need to explain the meaning of words and make the Bible understandable.

- They gave the meaning. What does this mean for us today? How does it apply to my life?

When we do this, people will understand the Bible. God's Word is always more powerful than any human word.

⁴ Ezra the teacher of the Law stood on a high wooden platform built for the occasion. Beside him on his right stood Mattithiah, Shema, Anaiah, Uriah, Hilkiah and Maaseiah; and on his left were Pedaiah, Mishael, Malkijah, Hashum, Hashbaddanah, Zechariah and Meshullam.⁵ Ezra opened the book. All the people could see him because he was standing above them; and as he opened it, the people all stood up. ⁶ Ezra praised the Lord, the great God; and all the people lifted their hands and responded, "Amen! Amen!" Then they bowed down and worshiped the Lord with their faces to the ground.

Second key to revival: Restoration of true worship

The Word of God was the center of this meeting. As they received the Word, worship flowed naturally, and there was respect, honor, and even fear of the Lord. The people stood up to listen to the Word. They do it in the Catholic church. Why don't we stand up to honor the Scripture?

- Ezra stood above them on a platform so all could see him, and to show respect. Today the pastor wears jeans, sits on a stool, and follows the latest fashions of the world. Of course he's also larger than life up on the giant screen. There's a reason why the pulpits in those old cathedrals were so high up. We've lost our awe of the Word and respect for the man who brings it to the people.

- Ezra was the first to praise the Lord. There was no band. It wasn't a concert. The priest led by example. I've been in many services where the pastor wasn't even present during the time of worship! Or he's preparing his message (a little late!), or talking with someone. The pastor should be the first to praise the Lord!

- There was a beautiful sense of reverence among the people, and everyone participated. I've noticed fewer and fewer people actually worshipping in churches. Some remain seated, others are busy with their phones (you can live without your phone for a couple hours!). People freely get up and walk in and out to use the bathroom or get a drink (or coffee from the Starbucks look-alike in the lobby). To many it's more a concert than something for them to participate in. There's need for instruction on what worship is all about. If they're not there to meet God, they're in the wrong place. There's a time for evangelistic concerts and outreaches,

but it's not during a worship service. God
deserves more.

- They were totally involved in the
  worship. Lifting their hands and bowing down
  with their faces to the ground. Worship is a very
  holy thing. God loves us, but he is awesome, and
  there are times when we should kneel in
  reverence.

What we have today in many churches is a circus. I find
myself asking: Where is Jesus? Often you hardly hear his
name. If we want revival we need to get back to the
Word, and true worship.

*9 Then Nehemiah the governor, Ezra the priest and
teacher of the Law, and the Levites who were instructing
the people said to them all, "This day is holy to the Lord
your God. Do not mourn or weep." For all the people had
been weeping as they listened to the words of the Law.*

Why were they crying? When we hear and understand
the Word it's like a glass of cold water, refreshing our
spirits and bringing tears. They may have been convicted
of their sins and failures as they heard the Word.
Perhaps they understood for the first time why they
went through the horrors of the exile. In various ways,
the Word touched them, and it will touch people in your
church like nothing else can.

This was a day set apart for the Lord (as every Lord's day should be). Yes, there was awe and reverence, but there should also be joy. We don't want to go back to funeral-like services. The joy of the Lord should fill the church. And the celebration will often include food:

[10] *Nehemiah said, "Go and enjoy choice food and sweet drinks, and send some to those who have nothing prepared. This day is holy to our Lord. Do not grieve, for the joy of the Lord is your strength."*

Third key: Restoration of the joy of the Lord through clear teaching of the Word and meaningful fellowship.

Nehemiah was used to good food and drink after years in the king's palace. He wasn't just a hard worker, he knew how to have a good time! There's nothing wrong with choice food and special drinks. God has given us food as a blessing to enjoy. (Maybe you should bring some "choice food" to the next pot luck?) Be sure to include people who have nothing prepared. Maybe send some of that pot luck meal to shut-ins?

It's in the context of a service that includes the Word, worship, and a common meal that we find the well-known verse: *The joy of the Lord is your strength.* Sadness saps our strength. If you're feeling weak, get to church. Get into the Lord's presence and praise him, and let his joy renew your strength.

[11]The Levites calmed all the people, saying, "Be still, for this is a holy day. Do not grieve." [12]Then all the people went away to eat and drink, to send portions of food and to celebrate with great joy, because they now understood the words that had been made known to them.

They were happy – because they understood the Word! What a shame that people often leave church confused, wondering what the message was all about. When we preach the Word in a way they can understand, there will be greater joy in the fellowship afterward.

[13]On the second day of the month, the heads of all the families, along with the priests and the Levites, gathered around Ezra the teacher to give attention to the words of the Law. [14]They found written in the Law, which the Lord had commanded through Moses, that the Israelites were to live in temporary shelters during the festival of the seventh month [15]and that they should proclaim this word and spread it throughout their towns and in Jerusalem: "Go out into the hill country and bring back branches from olive and wild olive trees, and from myrtles, palms and shade trees, to make temporary shelters"—as it is written.

[16]So the people went out and brought back branches and built themselves temporary shelters on their own roofs, in their courtyards, in the courts of the house of God and in the square by the Water Gate and the one by the Gate

of Ephraim. ¹⁷ The whole company that had returned from exile built temporary shelters and lived in them. From the days of Joshua son of Nun until that day, the Israelites had not celebrated it like this. And their joy was very great.

¹⁸ Day after day, from the first day to the last, Ezra read from the Book of the Law of God. They celebrated the festival for seven days, and on the eighth day, in accordance with the regulation, there was an assembly.

Fourth key to revival: Fathers taking their place in leadership, and together ensuring their families are obeying the Word.

There was another study the next day, but this time only the family heads (the fathers) took part. That's beautiful! Thank the Lord for godly women, but too often they take the lead, while God has called men to spiritual leadership. These men wanted to study all the details of the law to be sure they were obeying it, and they were all there so everyone was doing the same thing! It wasn't enough just to study – they took the lead in putting the Word into practice. In this case it meant celebrating the Feast of Booths (Sukkot). The purpose of the feast was to recall tent life in the desert during the Exodus. And the central part of their celebration? Hearing the Word of the Lord!

Under the leadership of the family heads, everyone participated. We need fathers that help the whole family obey the Word! And teachers who will work with those fathers to instruct them and help them do it! It's a great motivator to know all the other men are doing it!

Chapter 12

Two More Keys to Revival
Nehemiah 9

The revival started with the Word, worship, and fathers agreeing to bring their families in line with God's plan. This laid the foundation for the next step. It's great to worship, hear the Word, and make a commitment to obey it, but if there's still sin in our lives there will be no revival. When God's Spirit is moving, we see his holiness - and our sin. We can respond by hardening our hearts and continuing in sin, or by humbling ourselves. God calls us to genuine repentance, confessing our sin and changing our lives.

1On the twenty-fourth day of the same month, the Israelites gathered together, fasting and wearing sackcloth and putting dust on their heads. 2 Those of Israelite descent had separated themselves from all foreigners. They stood in their places and confessed their sins and the sins of their ancestors.

Fifth key to revival: Confession and repentance

After twenty-four days seeking the Lord they're ready to move on. What does genuine repentance involve?

Humbling themselves. When was the last time you fasted? In chapter eight we saw that God wants us to enjoy choice food, but there's also a time to deny ourselves. We're not too good at that. The flesh resists it. Fasting doesn't buy God's favor or obligate him to do something for us, but it does show God we're serious. It's a chance for self-examination and reflection. You see things more clearly when you're fasting. For the Jews, sackcloth and ashes were additional signs of mourning and humbling yourself. We don't do much sackcloth and ashes, but can you think of other ways we could show grief for our sin?

Sanctification. We hardly hear that word any more, and hardly practice what it means: separating ourselves from the world to live a holy life. Today everything is about prosperity and enjoying the things of the world, but God says anyone who chooses to be a friend of the world is his enemy (James 4:4). They separated themselves from all foreigners. There are things we have to separate from if we want revival. It doesn't necessarily mean they're all sinful. They may be fine in moderation. But if we're seeking God with all our hearts, we'll probably need to turn off the TV, the computer, and other distractions.

Confession

Publicly confessing your own sins. Did you think it was just Catholics who made confession, or that we should only confess sin to God? Remember James 5:16? *Therefore confess your sins to each other and pray for each other so that you may be healed.* A common characteristic of revivals through the centuries has been the public confession of sin. As one person confesses, others are moved to repentance. In a revival we no longer care about appearances. We just want God. We see how ugly our sin is and want to leave it behind. Be careful, however, about naming other people or sharing unnecessary details about your sin that draw attention to yourself.

Confessing the sins of your church, your country, and your ancestors. Like a priest, you intercede for God to have mercy and forgive those who have sinned. It's an important change in attitude. Instead of judging others, we're broken, and grieve over their sin, realizing we're part of that family, church, or country. To a certain extent, their sin is our sin. We identify with them.

[3] They stood where they were and read from the Book of the Law of the Lord their God for a quarter of the day, and spent another quarter in confession and in worshiping the Lord their God.

For seven days, every day, the whole group spent three hours reading the Bible, and then three hours responding to it in confession and worship. That's really allowing the Word to touch our hearts! How many people today would be ready to spend that much time before God?

⁴ Standing on the stairs of the Levites were Jeshua, Bani, Kadmiel, Shebaniah, Bunni, Sherebiah, Bani and Kenani. They cried out with loud voices to the Lord their God. ⁵ And the Levites—Jeshua, Kadmiel, Bani, Hashabneiah, Sherebiah, Hodiah, Shebaniah and Pethahiah—said: "Stand up and praise the Lord your God, who is from everlasting to everlasting"

Stand up and praise the Lord!

This is one of the most beautiful prayers in the Bible. Sixteen men cried out with loud voices, recounting all God had done for Israel. It's a great review of biblical history. Many biblical prayers speak of what God has done. Not that he doesn't know, but it serves as a foundation for our petitions, giving us perspective. The prayer is long, but don't just skip over it. Take some time to meditate on it, and pray it yourself.

⁵"Blessed be your glorious name, and may it be exalted above all blessing and praise. ⁶ You alone are the Lord. You made the heavens, even the highest heavens, and all their starry host, the earth and all that is on it, the seas and all that is in them. You give life to everything, and the multitudes of heaven worship you.

After all the humbling of themselves, it was time to praise the Lord. I love the picture of the multitudes of heaven worshipping God for his amazing creation. Does being in nature and seeing God's mighty acts move you to worship?

[15] In their hunger you gave them bread from heaven and in their thirst you brought them water from the rock; you told them to go in and take possession of the land you had sworn with uplifted hand to give them. [16] "But they, our ancestors, became arrogant and stiff-necked, and they did not obey your commands. [17] They refused to listen and failed to remember the miracles you performed among them. They became stiff-necked and in their rebellion appointed a leader in order to return to their slavery. But you are a forgiving God, gracious and compassionate, slow to anger and abounding in love. Therefore you did not desert them.

[26] "But they were disobedient and rebelled against you; they turned their backs on your law. They killed your prophets, who had warned them in order to turn them back to you; they committed awful blasphemies. [27] So you delivered them into the hands of their enemies, who oppressed them. But when they were oppressed they cried out to you. From heaven you heard them, and in

your great compassion you gave them deliverers, who rescued them from the hand of their enemies.

[28] *"But as soon as they were at rest, they again did what was evil in your sight. Then you abandoned them to the hand of their enemies so that they ruled over them. And when they cried out to you again, you heard from heaven, and in your compassion you delivered them time after time.*

God prospered them and gave them victory over their enemies, but unfortunately that don't necessarily keep us close to the Lord. Instead of being grateful and serving him, they responded by:

- Disobeying.
- Rebelling.
- Rejecting his Word.
- Killing his prophets.
- Committing awful blasphemies.

God can't allow that rebellion, so he punishes them by handing them over to enemies who oppress them.

We often have to hit rock bottom before we cry out to God. And because he's so merciful and compassionate, he listens, and sends deliverers to free us. But does it lead to genuine repentance? Frequently, as soon as things get better, we go right back to our sin. Israel did, so they handed over to their enemies again. And they cried out to God, who delivered them. And so it goes, over and over. Unfortunately, it's the life story of many Christians. If you've been caught in that vicious cycle, God wants to deliver you.

[29] *"You warned them in order to turn them back to your law, but they became arrogant and disobeyed your commands. They sinned against your ordinances, of which you said, 'The person who obeys them will live by them.' Stubbornly they turned their backs on you, became stiff-necked and refused to listen.* [30] *For many years you were patient with them. By your Spirit you warned them through your prophets. Yet they paid no attention, so you gave them into the hands of the neighboring peoples.* [31] *But in your great mercy you did not put an end to them or abandon them, for you are a gracious and merciful God.*

As we succumb to sin, God sends prophets and pastors to warn us through his Spirit. Because of God's great patience, we may continue in our rebellious ways for years, mistakenly thinking we've escaped God's judgment. If we choose to repent, God will be gracious to us. Israel never did. Instead of softening their hearts in response to God's love and mercy, like so many of us, they:

- Became arrogant.
- Disobeyed his Word.
- Stubbornly turned their backs on God.
- Became stiff-necked.

- Refused to listen.
- Paid no attention to warnings.

So once again they fall in the hands of their enemies, but even in judgment God is gracious and merciful. He doesn't abandon you or destroy you. He always wants your restoration.

32 "Now therefore, our God, the great God, mighty and awesome, who keeps his covenant of love, do not let all this hardship seem trifling in your eyes—the hardship that has come on us, on our kings and leaders, on our priests and prophets, on our ancestors and all your people, from the days of the kings of Assyria until today. 33 In all that has happened to us, you have remained righteous; you have acted faithfully, while we acted wickedly. 34 Our kings, our leaders, our priests and our ancestors did not follow your law; they did not pay attention to your commands or the statutes you warned them to keep. 35 Even while they were in their kingdom, enjoying your great goodness to them in the spacious and fertile land you gave them, they did not serve you or turn from their evil ways.

They can finally see how their sin and their ancestors' sin has destroyed them. Yet despite their repentance and prayers, they're still suffering:

36 "But see, we are slaves today, slaves in the land you gave our ancestors so they could eat its fruit and the other good things it produces. *37 Because of our sins, its abundant harvest goes to the kings you have placed over us. They rule over our bodies and our cattle as they please. We are in great distress.*

They're back in their land, but it's a mess, and they're still slaves. Others are enjoying the fruit of their labors. They've lost almost everything. Do you know what that's like? Maybe in prison? Or under crushing financial burdens? It takes faith to keep believing, to keep pressing in and trusting God. They've spent seven days confessing their sin. Now, what's the next step?

38 "In view of all this, we are making a binding agreement, putting it in writing, and our leaders, our Levites and our priests are affixing their seals to it."

Sixth key for revival: It starts with the leaders. Join together and make a serious commitment to serving the Lord together and leading his people in obedience.

If there's any hope of maintaining the progress they've made and pressing into all God has for them, the leadership must be faithful to God's Word and care for the people God has entrusted to them. They make a covenant, a binding agreement, and sign and seal it.

They've come a long way. This has been an amazing outpouring of prayer, worship, and commitment. But there's still two more keys to experiencing genuine revival.

Chapter 13

Two Final Keys to Revival
Nehemiah 10

When the leaders get serious about obeying the Lord, the people follow:

[28] "The rest of the people—priests, Levites, gatekeepers, musicians, temple servants and all who separated themselves from the neighboring peoples for the sake of the Law of God, together with their wives and all their sons and daughters who are able to understand— [29] all these now join their fellow Israelites the nobles, and bind themselves with a curse and an oath to follow the Law of God given through Moses the servant of God and to obey carefully all the commands, regulations and decrees of the Lord our Lord.

Seventh key to revival: As a body of believers, make a public commitment to obey the Lord and live according to his Word.

Nehemiah was the first to place his seal on the covenant. All the other leaders followed. But unless the people wholeheartedly make the same commitment, there will be no revival. To change the course of the nation they must also think about their children. In most revivals the next generation loses the parents' fervor or leaves the church. They had a good start. The fathers had already met to study the Word and were working together to help their families live it. Obviously there's no way to guarantee a faith that lasts, but too often fathers fail to take their place of authority and say "this is a Christian home and we're going to live according to God's Word here." Then, most importantly, he lives it, as a servant willing to lay down his life for his family. Do you think that's something God wants you to do? Do you have brothers who will join you?

In the past, public commitments were made in baptisms, confirmation, and church membership. Today, few want to make those commitments, even the commitment of marriage. And they don't keep them. When a marriage doesn't seem to be working they look for an easy out. Instead of committing to a local body of Christ, they run from church to church.

This wasn't about the emotion of the moment. It was a step of obedience. To maintain revival we must move beyond emotion (without losing it), to a decision of the will to follow Christ and obey his Word come what may. Family heads and church leaders set the example of faithfulness to that commitment.

30 "We promise not to give our daughters in marriage to the peoples around us or take their daughters for our sons.

I'm amazed at how many Christians don't seem to know that the Bible commands us not to date or marry unbelievers. Countless homes and Christians have been destroyed because they've ignored that clear biblical teaching. If you're single, decide now you will not date or marry anyone who is not a dedicated disciple of Jesus Christ.

31 "When the neighboring peoples bring merchandise or grain to sell on the Sabbath, we will not buy from them on the Sabbath or on any holy day. Every seventh year we will forgo working the land and will cancel all debts.

What's more important? God or money? Your business or your spiritual life? Here they promise to place God first. Unfortunately, Christian businessmen frequently fail to bring their faith into their business. The owners of Chick-fil-A and Hobby Lobby have lost millions because they won't open on Sundays, but God honors that commitment. A true revival will touch the business world.

32 "We assume the responsibility for carrying out the commands to give a third of a shekel each year for the service of the house of our God: 33 for the bread set out on the table; for the regular grain offerings and burnt offerings; for the offerings on the Sabbaths, at the New Moon feasts and at the appointed festivals; for the holy offerings; for sin offering to make atonement for Israel; and for all the duties of the house of our God.

[34] "We—the priests, the Levites and the people—have cast lots to determine when each of our families is to bring to the house of our God at set times each year a contribution of wood to burn on the altar of the Lord our God, as it is written in the Law.

[35] "We also assume responsibility for bringing to the house of the Lord each year the firstfruits of our crops and of every fruit tree.

[36] "As it is also written in the Law, we will bring the firstborn of our sons and of our cattle, of our herds and of our flocks to the house of our God, to the priests ministering there.

[37] "Moreover, we will bring to the storerooms of the house of our God, to the priests, the first of our ground meal, of our grain offerings, of the fruit of all our trees and of our new wine and olive oil. And we will bring a tithe of our crops to the Levites, for it is the Levites who collect the tithes in all the towns where we work. [38] A priest descended from Aaron is to accompany the Levites when they receive the tithes, and the Levites are to bring a tenth of the tithes up to the house of our God, to the storerooms of the treasury. [39] The people of Israel,

including the Levites, are to bring their contributions of grain, new wine and olive oil to the storerooms, where the articles for the sanctuary and for the ministering priests, the gatekeepers and the musicians are also kept.

Eighth key: Get the focus off ourselves and our prosperity, and give to the worldwide work of the Gospel

Real revival touches our personal finances. Many Christians live under crushing debt while trying to maintain lavish lifestyles. Unfortunately, many churches promote it. Few tithe, which is actually an Old Testament requirement. Christ teaches that *everything* belongs to God, who then provides what we need to live on. God wants to free us from debt and the heretical teaching of self-centered prosperity. There are brothers and sisters all over the world doing amazing things for the Lord. Many don't even have bicycles or horses to visit churches they've planted, while we're asking God for a new luxury car. Today we have excellent opportunities to help them.

[39] *"We will not neglect the house of our God."*

One of Israel's sins at that time was neglecting God's house while building beautiful homes for themselves (Haggai 1). I believe neglecting God's house includes neglecting anything that has to do with his work. We neglect his house when we have big, beautiful, church buildings, while brothers on the other side of town or other side of the world don't even have a building. Do everything possible to make sure his whole house is well supplied, with adequate (though not ostentatious) facilities, and everything needed to advance the Kingdom.

Chapter 14

A People for God
Nehemiah 12 & 13

In the first chapter of Haggai, the prophet explains the consequences of misplaced priorities and neglecting God's house. Nothing was working. The people were leading frustrated, empty, lives. In Nehemiah 10 and 11 the leaders and the whole nation promise to follow all God's law, not marry foreigners, and care for God's temple. The people seemed to have learned their lesson. Witnessing the near total destruction of their country and spending so many years in slavery should motivate them to live right.

But that wasn't the case. We have short memories, because in Nehemiah 13:11 once again they were neglecting God's house. It's so easy for us to neglect the things of God, especially when we're doing well. How did it happen, even under Nehemiah's capable leadership?

The walls dedicated

In Nehemiah 12 the walls of Jerusalem were dedicated. It was a day of great rejoicing:

²⁷ At the dedication of the wall of Jerusalem, the Levites were sought out from where they lived and were brought to Jerusalem to celebrate joyfully the dedication with songs of thanksgiving and with the music of cymbals, harps and lyres. ³⁰ When the priests and Levites had purified themselves ceremonially, they purified the people, the gates and the wall. ³¹ I had the leaders of Judah go up on top of the wall. I also assigned two large choirs to give thanks. One was to proceed on top of the wall to the right.⁴³ And on that day they offered great sacrifices, rejoicing because God had given them great joy. The women and children also rejoiced. The sound of rejoicing in Jerusalem could be heard far away.

What a glorious conclusion to the months of hard labor! After the worship and praise, the first thing they turned to was the Scripture, and God has a fresh word for them. There's something important that had escaped their attention (13:1):

On that day the Book of Moses was read aloud in the hearing of the people and there it was found written that no Ammonite or Moabite should ever be admitted into the assembly of God, ² because they had not met the Israelites with food and water but had hired Balaam to call a curse down on them. (Our God, however, turned the curse into a blessing.)

What a merciful God we have, who turns curses into blessings! May he turn any curse against you or your family into a blessing! But now they had a big problem. In the midst of their celebration they realized some of the people had no business being there. In fact, God was offended by their presence! It may seem harsh, but God does have the right to decide who can and cannot enter his kingdom. Today there is tremendous pressure to be tolerant and accept everyone, regardless of their sin or lifestyle. But if you read the Bible you'll find out it wasn't just the Ammonites and Moabites who were excluded. For example, I Corinthians 6:9-10:

Or do you not know that wrongdoers will not inherit the kingdom of God? Do not be deceived: Neither the sexually immoral nor idolaters nor adulterers nor men who have sex with men ^{nor} thieves nor the greedy nor drunkards nor slanderers nor swindlers will inherit the kingdom of God.

Or Revelation 22:15:

Outside are the dogs, those who practice magic arts, the sexually immoral, the murderers, the idolaters and everyone who loves and practices falsehood.

The only acceptable response to sin is to repent and make things right with God and others. Twenty five years earlier (Ezra 10:3), in a similar situation, they expelled the foreign wives and their children. It can be very painful and costly to repent. But it's even more costly – eternally so – to continue in sin.

A holy people

³ *When the people heard this law, they excluded from Israel all who were of foreign descent.*

Rebuilding the walls of Jerusalem could easily be seen as a lifetime accomplishment. Add the excitement of the tremendous worship and hearing God's voice, and Nehemiah could have felt very satisfied.

But he knew that was not enough.

Spearheading an impressive building program and leading a church known for great preaching and powerful worship would mean success for many pastors.

But unless there's a body of believers serious about holiness and putting the Word in practice, that house will be built on sand and won't last (Matthew 7:24-27).

Nehemiah had seen the glories of Solomon's temple and lived in a prosperous Jerusalem. And he saw it destroyed because the people embraced an empty religiosity and failed to obey God's Word.

He would not rest until he's done all he could to ensure his people were walking with the Lord. That's the heart of a true servant of Jesus, much more than buildings, great music, or even great preaching.

When are we going to wake up and boldly cleanse the Body of Christ of the sin that is bound to bring God's judgment, and get serious about obedience?

This wasn't the only problem, either:

4 Before this, Eliashib the priest had been put in charge of the storerooms of the house of our God. He was closely associated with Tobiah, 5 and he had provided him with a large room formerly used to store the grain offerings and incense and temple articles, and also the tithes of grain, new wine and olive oil prescribed for the Levites, musicians and gatekeepers, as well as the contributions for the priests.

Remember Tobiah? He was one of Nehemiah's archenemies – and an enemy of God's people. And he was an Ammonite. He could care less about the Jews and had no part in worshipping God. He was an evil man. But the high priest's son had married Tobiah's best friend's daughter, and the two had become tight. So tight that Tobiah was given space right in the temple of God, in what was supposed to be a storeroom for temple articles.

Are you aware there are wolves in sheep's clothing in the church? Do you know that enemies of the Gospel would love to make their way in among the elders and worship team to be used by the devil? We need much discernment. Often family, convenience, and personal benefit influence our decisions too much.

Nehemiah takes a vacation

Nehemiah would never have allowed this to happen, but he had to go back to see the king in Babylon, and all kinds of havoc broke out while he was gone. Remember Aaron and the golden calf when Moses was on the mountain? Be careful if you have to be away from the church for a while. The wolf is waiting for the pastor to leave to jump on the sheep.

[6] But while all this was going on, I was not in Jerusalem, for in the thirty-second year of Artaxerxes king of Babylon I had returned to the king. Some time later I asked his permission [7] and came back to Jerusalem. Here I learned about the evil thing Eliashib had done in providing Tobiah a room in the courts of the house of God. [8] I was greatly displeased and threw all Tobiah's household goods out of the room. [9] I gave orders to purify the rooms, and then I put back into them the equipment of the house of God, with the grain offerings and the incense.

It's always easier to put someone into leadership than get rid of them. It's easier to give someone a room in the temple to gain their favor than to get them out of that room. But when something profane enters the church we have to get rid of it, purify the church, and set things in godly order.

10 I also learned that the portions assigned to the Levites had not been given to them, and that all the Levites and musicians responsible for the service had gone back to their own fields. 11 So I rebuked the officials and asked them, "Why is the house of God neglected?" Then I called them together and stationed them at their posts.

The people weren't providing for the priests and musicians, so they got discouraged and went back to their fields. God established authority and leadership in the church for a reason. As soon as Nehemiah left, things started falling apart. Our tendency is to forget about God's work and go back to our fields. We need someone like Nehemiah to motivate us and keep us obedient to the Word. You may be tired of trying to keep things together, but you may be a Nehemiah. Don't give up! Your task is never easy! If you feel like you're not getting adequate support and want to go back to your fields, remember it's God you're serving, and he's the one who called you.

12 All Judah brought the tithes of grain, new wine and olive oil into the storerooms. 13 I put Shelemiah the priest, Zadok the scribe, and a Levite named Pedaiah in charge of the storerooms and made Hanan son of Zakkur, the son of Mattaniah, their assistant, because they were considered trustworthy. They were made responsible for distributing the supplies to their fellow Levites.

Maybe Nehemiah didn't have the chance to do this earlier, but now he names trustworthy men to be in charge. Look for trustworthy men to help you. You won't always be around. One measure of your success as a leader is the church's ability to keep going when you're not there.

[14] Remember me for this, my God, and do not blot out what I have so faithfully done for the house of my God and its services.

Nehemiah was a man of prayer, and we see him talking with God over and over in this book – not just in his prayer closet, but throughout the day. It was a natural part of his life. May God remember all that you have faithfully done for his house!

Desecrating the Sabbath

[15] In those days I saw people in Judah treading winepresses on the Sabbath and bringing in grain and loading it on donkeys, together with wine, grapes, figs and all other kinds of loads. And they were bringing all this into Jerusalem on the Sabbath. Therefore I warned them against selling food on that day. [16] People from Tyre who lived in Jerusalem were bringing in fish and all kinds of merchandise and selling them in Jerusalem on the Sabbath to the people of Judah. [17] I rebuked the

nobles of Judah and said to them, "What is this wicked thing you are doing—desecrating the Sabbath day? [18] Didn't your ancestors do the same things, so that our God brought all this calamity on us and on this city? Now you are stirring up more wrath against Israel by desecrating the Sabbath."

[19] When evening shadows fell on the gates of Jerusalem before the Sabbath, I ordered the doors to be shut and not opened until the Sabbath was over. I stationed some of my own men at the gates so that no load could be brought in on the Sabbath day. [20] Once or twice the merchants and sellers of all kinds of goods spent the night outside Jerusalem. [21] But I warned them and said, "Why do you spend the night by the wall? If you do this again, I will arrest you." From that time on they no longer came on the Sabbath. [22] Then I commanded the Levites to purify themselves and go and guard the gates in order to keep the Sabbath day holy.

They had promised to keep the Sabbath (10:31), but are quickly breaking their promise. It seems like businessmen always look for a way to make money. They may try to organize the church like a business and sell things there, but the church isn't a business, and we need to make sure the things of God are kept holy. Some would say that Nehemiah was too controlling, even trying to play cop. But Nehemiah knew the fear of the Lord. Some of the youngsters may have forgotten the devastation of the exile, but he knew that you can't play with God. We need to be zealous about holiness and worshipping God!

Remember me for this also, my God, and show mercy to me according to your great love.

Why would Nehemiah ask God to show him mercy? Because what he was doing was hard! It wasn't easy to confront all these people! He had to continually remind himself why he was doing it and draw strength from God's great love. Standing up for Christ and leading his people is hard work!

Mixed marriages

23 Moreover, in those days I saw men of Judah who had married women from Ashdod, Ammon and Moab. 24 Half of their children spoke the language of Ashdod or the language of one of the other peoples, and did not know how to speak the language of Judah. 25 I rebuked them and called curses down on them. I beat some of the men and pulled out their hair. I made them take an oath in God's name and said: "You are not to give your daughters in marriage to their sons, nor are you to take their daughters in marriage for your sons or for yourselves. 26 Was it not because of marriages like these that Solomon king of Israel sinned? Among the many nations there was no king like him. He was loved by his God, and God made him king over all Israel, but even he was led into sin by foreign women. 27 Must we hear now that you too are doing all this terrible wickedness and are being unfaithful to our God by marrying foreign women?"

They had also promised not to marry foreign women (10:30). We're unfaithful to God if we enter into the holy covenant of marriage with someone who doesn't know Jesus. Twenty-five years earlier, Ezra pulled out his own hair because of this same situation (Ezra 9:3), but Nehemiah is a little more forceful. He beat them and pulled out *their* hair!

Don't go back to your sin! It's easy to make promises to God, especially when things are rough or you're pressured by others in the church. But God will judge you even more severely if you go back to your sin, and you open yourself to worse demonic oppression.

28 One of the sons of Joiada son of Eliashib the high priest was son-in-law to Sanballat the Horonite. And I drove him away from me.

Sanballat was another enemy of Nehemiah and the Jews, but he had arranged for his daughter to marry the high priest's son. Nehemiah couldn't tolerate that, and even though it was politically risky and unpopular, he drove the young man away. He had to give an example to the rest of the people.

29 Remember them, my God, because they defiled the priestly office and the covenant of the priesthood and of the Levites.

30 So I purified the priests and the Levites of everything foreign, and assigned them duties, each to his own task. 31 I also made provision for contributions of wood at designated times, and for the firstfruits.

Nehemiah knew how important it was to carefully follow God's Word. Being a leader in God's church is a serious calling. Very carefully, after much prayer, assign duties to leaders and properly organize the work of the church. We neglect God's work if we leave the church unorganized and without proper leadership.

Remember me with favor, my God.

In all he's done, Nehemiah hasn't looked for recognition in this world. He built no great monument in his honor. The wall was never named the Nehemiah Memorial Wall. We remember him for his book and one of the greatest examples of godly leadership. But most important for Nehemiah was to be remembered by God. The Lord assures a great reward to those who faithfully serve him. May you follow Nehemiah in zealous, uncompromising, service to your God. Rebuild the walls! Close the gates! Help prepare a spotless bride for our Lord Jesus Christ!

Conclusion

Will You Stand in the Gap?

Nehemiah was the answer to a great dilemma God faced many years earlier. Yes, God Almighty, the Lord of the universe, faces dilemmas. Before the judgment and exile to Babylon, the whole nation, including prophets, priests, and rulers, are deep in sin. God has been patient, but now his anger is so great he can't tolerate any more. He must destroy them. But he still hesitates. He loves them so much and longs to spare them, see them repent, and restore them. It's still possible, but he needs someone who will intercede and stand in the gap for them. For some reason that we don't fully understand, he has chosen to work through us, his creation. But he found no one available to do the job. We read about it in Ezekiel 22.

[23]Again the word of the Lord came to me: [24] "Son of man, say to the land, 'You are a land that has not been cleansed or rained on in the day of wrath.' [25] There is a conspiracy of her princes within her like a roaring lion tearing its prey; they devour people, take treasures and precious things and make many widows within her. [26] Her priests do violence to my law and profane my holy

things; they do not distinguish between the holy and the common; they teach that there is no difference between the unclean and the clean; and they shut their eyes to the keeping of my Sabbaths, so that I am profaned among them. [27] Her officials within her are like wolves tearing their prey; they shed blood and kill people to make unjust gain. [28] Her prophets whitewash these deeds for them by false visions and lying divinations. They say, 'This is what the Sovereign Lord says'—when the Lord has not spoken. [29] The people of the land practice extortion and commit robbery; they oppress the poor and needy and mistreat the foreigner, denying them justice.

Every part of the nation reflects absolute corruption:

The land

The New Living Translation says it's *a polluted land.* It's dirty and can't be cleansed because of the continuing sin. It's also dry. The very land is experiencing the consequences of the peoples' sin as God's wrath is poured out on it. Ezekiel is to *speak* to the land!

The princes

They put people to death, then steal everything of value. Husbands are killed, and many women are left as widows. (CEV) The Greek Septuagint Old Testament calls them princes, but the original Hebrew says *prophets.* They may have been false prophets who had gotten involved in politics. They've entered into a conspiracy, and, like the devil, steal, kill, and destroy, as a roaring lion tearing its prey.

The priests

Instead of modeling obedience, honoring God's law, and teaching the people to do the same, they do violence and profane God's holy things (GNT: *break my law and have no respect for what is holy*), from the temple and religious observances, to marriage and sexuality. They fail to differentiate between the holy and the common, loving the world and embracing all it offers. No guidance is given to the people on right and wrong or clean and unclean. As a result, God is profaned among the people. He is not honored, revered, or feared. Their religion has become a joke.

The officials

Those in authority are like wolves tearing their prey, shedding blood and killing people for unjust gain.

The prophets

The very ones who should be exposing sin cover it with lies, *pretending to have received visions and special revelations* (CEV). They give false assurance to the people that everything is okay and God is pleased with them, claiming to speak in the name of the Lord, when God has been silent. We must be very careful of false prophets today!

The people

Following their leaders' example, the people extort, rob, and oppress the poor and needy. As in the US today, the rich get richer and lack concern for the poor, who are sinking further into poverty. They mistreat foreigners and deny them justice. God cares for the "undocumented!" We must be careful of how we treat immigrants! Instead of being our brother's keeper, we are consumed with looking out for our own welfare.

Will you stand in the gap?

No one would deny this is a desperate situation, well deserving of God's judgment. His justice demands that he does something! But he still loves them, and here's his dilemma:

30 "I looked for someone among them who would build up the wall and stand before me in the gap on behalf of the land so I would not have to destroy it, but I found no one. 31 So I will pour out my wrath on them and consume them with my fiery anger, bringing down on their own heads all they have done, declares the Sovereign Lord."

God was looking for someone to build the wall and fill in the gaps. It took a long time, long after the judgment and destruction of Jerusalem, but he finally found a righteous man! That's exactly what Nehemiah did!

Eventually God himself provided someone to permanently fill that gap. Our Lord Jesus Christ is the perfect high priest! All God's wrath was poured out on Jesus on the cross. He stood in the gap. If you've drifted away from the Lord or have never given your life to Jesus, he's ready to forgive your sin and give you a new life. Make this your prayer:

Lord Jesus, I believe that you died to pay for my sin, rose from the dead, and are living today. I give you my life. Forgive me, cleanse me, and give me a new life. I want to follow you and serve you as my Lord. Fill me with your Holy Spirit. Thank you for your salvation. Amen.

God still needs intercessors today; men and women willing to stand in the gap out of love for God and his people. He needs someone who will rebuild the protective walls of righteousness around his people. Nehemiah has given us a great example. There is much we can learn from him about leadership. It's amazing what that one man did. It doesn't take large numbers for God to work. He can do miracles through you, but it won't be easy. Are you available?